TESTI

D1650372

"If you thought social media was all about clicks, likes and follows, think again. Katie will help you to create soulcial media – soul-filled social media and content that creates community, that feels real to produce and to receive, and the good news is, there's not a wanky countdown clock or old-paradigm click-bait sales technique in sight. Hurrah. Katie gives us all permission to take a collective sigh of relief and encourages us to do social media on our terms – if you're a conscious human who uses social media in any way, you NEED this book."

– Lisa Lister, author of
Love Your Lady Landscape and *Witch*

"Prepare for success as Katie my Social Media Angel shares her wisdom. This book is about the importance of using social media to create community and connection to help the ascension of planet. A social spiritual movement as well as a practical guide for helping your business to fly online, as mine has working with her."

– Diana Cooper, author of *Archangel Guide to Ascension* and *Archangel Guide to Enlightenment and Mastery: Living In The Fifth Dimension*

"Katie has embraced the wholeness of what social media is. She knows it is more than a technique. She proves/witnesses that it is a connective tissue between our souls and she will guide you to let your true spirit express and communicate to the world. She is all about honesty, truth, soul language and expression of love. She will facilitate you to discover how to reach your true communication to the world and then enjoy the journey rather being trapped in a tight egotistical road that can attract us on the web. Be yourself is her motto! I know her pure and joyful heart will guide you in her book. And you will so enjoy it!"

Karen Ruimy, author of the
Voice of The Angel & founder of *Kalmar*.

"Katie Brockhurst lovingly supports the co-creation of authentic online conversations, keeping you pointed towards your north as you navigate the ever-evolving world of social media, human led algorithms and changes in content consciousness. She adds to the conversation, recognising the research and knowledge which served us previously, moving towards the waves of fresh development in a very real online world. This book will guide you with ease and grace, humour and love."

– Gail Love Schock,
Heart Brain Coherence Mentor

"Do you want an actual angel of a person to help you make sense of how to use social media with integrity, authenticity and joy? That's Katie and this book is it. Before working with Katie, we were pretty low-key panicked about using social media in our business: it felt awkward, stuffy, overwhelming, inauthentic, and actually scary. As a result, we pretty much didn't use social media (bummer) and built up stress from feeling like social media failures. Katie utterly transformed our relationship to social media, coaching us to step into sharing our authentic voices on social media, and building our community online: we grew from 1000 followers to 10,000 in 3 months simply by using her techniques to reach out and share. Social media now feels like a place of peace, authenticity, and connection… How crazy is that? :) We've got a plan and a structure to support us, and yet we flow and let ourselves be inspired. We know that we can be our authentic selves online, and that's the best way to serve, so we don't hit overwhelm anymore. It's the best! "

– Eliza and Sil Reynolds, authors of,
Mothering and Daughtering

"Katie's soulful and authentic approach to social media is unique and refreshing in a world where likes and followers rule. With Katie's guidance I reconnected with the soul of my online presence and learned to micromanage the energy and intention I'm putting into my posts. This was crucial for me!"

– Christine Wheeler, author of
Tapping for Teenage Girls

"Rather than providing you with set formulas and techniques, Katie encourages you to get clear on who you are and what your brand stands for, and use this information to create an authentic and personalised social media strategy. Katie has helped me to develop more emotional & relationship-building content, which has made it more approachable, fun and ultimately more effective!"

– George Lizos, author of
Be The Guru

"I love Katie's unique, inspiring and thought-provoking ways of working with social media - completely different to everyone else in the industry - in a way that completely spoke to my heart. She challenges me to think outside the box not only with my social media but my entire business! This is not about boosting numbers and playing the vanity game but really connecting with your customers in a way only you can. Katie brings so much joy to the whole process."

– Nicola Salmon,
coach & founder of *Fertility Freedom*

This edition is published by
That Guy's House in 2018

www.ThatGuysHouse.com

SOCIAL MEDIA FOR A
NEW AGE

Simple strategies that are authentic and true,
passionate, real, in alignment with YOU.

KATIE BROCKHURST

hey,

Welcome to this wonderful book brought to you by That Guy's House Publishing.

At That Guy's House we believe in real and raw wellness books that inspire the reader from a place of authenticity and honesty.

This book has been carefully crafted by both the author and publisher with the intention that it will bring you a glimmer of hope, a rush of inspiration and sensation of inner peace.

It is our hope that you thoroughly enjoy this book and pass it onto friends who may also be in need of a glimpse into their own magnificence.

Have a wonderful day.

Love,

Sean Patrick
That Guy.

TABLE OF CONTENTS

THE PROLOGUE

Social Media for a New Age,
Is the next stage,
in how we engage.
When we raise the vibration,
And have some fun,
much more than likes and follows,
are ours to be won.

Social media is playing a big part in the evolution of our consciousness. Both on a personal level and as a collective, it's bringing us together on a global scale.

On the macro it is being used for the greater good, quickly spreading awareness of social causes and movements such as #metoo and #blacklivesmatter. On the micro level, it is a place of connection between friends, family, businesses and communities of all kind.

I've worked in social media for over a decade now, and I've had the opportunity to work with people who want to use it to build meaningful platforms to support and showcase their businesses, projects, missions and causes. This has given me a unique perspective and direct insight into how it works and how it can be used to create and serve your life, your business and your communities. I also have my own unique approach to social media, which I want to share with you. I wanted to create something reassuring and inspiring that will help more people traverse, dance and feel at ease with this ever-evolving multidimensional digital landscape we now find ourselves immersed in.

As a digital, modern and global society we have gone past the point of no return when considering if we are able to, or want to, totally unplug from what is now our reality. Yes, we can learn how to manage our time online better, but social and digital media is impacting all areas of our lives now. It is a very recent development in our evolution and we are but teenagers of a digital revolution. As we mature, it is something we can and will have to become more conscious of; how we are being affected by it and how effectively we use it.

The digital world may technically be artificial, yet, we are the ones that have created it, we are the ones continuing to develop and code it, and we are the ones uploading to it and supplying it with information. It's a symbiotic relationship, with social media in many ways being a total reflection of us.

We say we want to be the change we want to see in the world, and I believe that each of us has the capacity to effect positive change for ourselves, for each other and for the planet by using social media in a more conscious and effective way.

In this book, I will be sharing with you some of what I have seen, learnt, experienced and developed during my 10+ years of being online professionally, creating digital media for both myself and clients and through supporting many different authors, teachers and practitioners in the spiritual and wellness sphere to create online platforms.

One of my clients and Instagram family @lucyannechard, shared on Instagram recently:

"For soul-led, heart-centred guidance on anything social media related follow @katiekdot_ socialmediaangel. This fabulous woman helped me totally rebuild my relationship with social media and trust my inner wisdom when it comes to sharing my voice online".

I hope that this book and what I share in it, can go some way to doing the same for you.

This is not a 'how to' do social media marketing book. While it *does* contain practical support, insight and ideas to help you manage your social media presence as a tool to support your business (in a creative, soulful and spiritual way), its main intention is to create a thought-provoking conversation about social media for the new age.

Why?

So that together we may discover a new, more enjoyable and more effective way to use social media to create, innovate and share.

During the writing of this book, I've been in conversation with people, peers and clients who are looking for a new and different way to use social media. They tell me of the product launches and Facebook ad campaigns that have not gone the way they had hoped, or been sold. About how much time and energy has been put into creating lead magnets, sales pages and big fancy launches, using digital marketing methods and formulas that are famed for their 'success', but that haven't worked for them. They share with me how they have lost money, time and more importantly, confidence trying to use social media in this formulaic, cookie-cutter way to market their businesses.

I've written this book for people who know the potential of social media, but don't want to lose themselves in scrolling, comparison and doing what the so-called experts tell them to do. I've written it for anyone that's ever asked on a client call *surely, there's got to be another way?* I've written it for those working within the Mind, Body, Spirit field, for all the authors and budding authors, wellness practitioners, for all the witches, the magicians, the fae folk, the mermaids and mermen, and let us not forget the unicorns.

It is for those of us who are using social media to share our magic, our ideas, our services and our art… Connecting, sharing and healing the world with our brothers and sisters from rainbow tribes all across Gaia.

PERSONAL, SUBJECTIVE AND UNIQUE

Throughout the book, you will see me repeat that being online (and offline for that matter) is **personal, subjective and unique**. This is one of the core concepts of Social Media For A New Age and it's important, for they are also the very words that Facebook Inc. use to describe their core newsfeed values.

Showing up on social media is a journey we all embark on when we choose to use it, when we choose to become visible, when we choose to be seen online in order to support and share our projects, businesses and dreams with the world.

Like the tip of the iceberg, though, we often don't see what is underneath. A 'quick fix to success' myth is perpetuated and sold to us by the very nature of social media which shows off highlight reels, glossy Instagram grids and

Facebook feeds, which are often masking reality and the truth behind what it takes to create (or even have) a business of value. We don't see the years of hard work involved in developing a skill or a trade, the mistakes made along the way or the sleepless nights that many entrepreneurs or small business owners have been through to get to where they are now.

"Building a business with heart and dreams takes time, a long time of research, time to make juicy mistakes and money saved up over years, patience, being in it for the long haul, building slow, steady relationships... Yes, it looks juicy on a Facebook feed, but the beauty takes time and energy." Clare Jasmine Beloved on Facebook @clarejasminebeloved

We also don't see the big budgets, the teams, the expertise and mastermind groups that have gone into creating some of the platforms that we see online that we then compare ourselves to.

It is all **personal, subjective and unique.**

It is a bit (a lot) of a minefield out there in terms of the sheer amount of information available about what to do and how to BE online, what is defined as success (how to create a six-figure business, how to launch a programme etc.) and because of all this information about 'success' and what you *should* be doing to achieve it, it can become confusing for us on many different levels.

Many people will come to social media with the big expectation that success online and offline will be fast and easy. An outside-in rather than inside-out approach, that makes us think creating a pretty social media grid and getting lots of followers is what it takes to create a sustainable, long term business.

This confusion can then lead to all sorts of issues, where we feel disillusioned, frustrated and give up on social media, due to the false expectations we have of it. This is also where relationship problems with social media can arise, including addiction, self-criticism and depression.

I want this book to be social media medicine, an antidote to all of the information that is not in alignment with your souls way of being, so that you can find your own way of using social media, in a way that is ***personal, subjective and unique*** to you.

And it isn't just about how we use social media either, more often than not, it's about US and where we are currently at. This can express itself through lots of the different fears (False Evidence Appearing Real) that social media brings up for many of us.

Fear of being seen.
Fear of having nothing (worthy) to say or share.
Fear that we are a bit crap (or definitely not as good as him or her.)
Fear of being in a leadership role / a leader.
Fear of not getting 'likes' (reach or engagement…)
"What if nobody or not enough people 'like' me?"
Fear of being judged (for that and for everything else)
Fear of being different.
Fear of being misunderstood.
Fear of the ever-changing technology (especially amongst non-natives.)
Fear that we are boring people.
Spamming people.
Showing off too much to people.
Being too salesy.
Pushy…
Inauthentic.
Fear of being too much.
Too little.
Too big.
Too fat.
Too pretty.
Too ugly.
Too skinny.
Too everything.
Fear… Fear… Fear…
All of the above… And some.

I call this the **social media vortex of doom.**

There are many ways to do, and to be on social media, and honestly? Social media isn't for everyone. If you're not just using it for personal reasons and you *are* using it to share your art, skills, gifts and talents with the world it will demand that you show up and share yourself, your thoughts and your ideas.

If you ARE going to use it this way, it's best to believe in it, commit to it and be consistent with it. (Except for when you're not. More on that later.) It will require resources in the form of your time, energy, enthusiasm, LOVE and yes, sometimes money too.

I am infusing this book with my understanding and belief that you will be rewarded for your brave efforts and intention in showing up on social media. That by connecting with others openly, by sharing yourself, your creativity, your joy, your wisdom, knowledge, LOVE and vulnerability, in an authentic way, sends out a message to the universe that you are ready, willing and able to receive from it in return.

NOTE: It may not reward you directly with likes, clicks and sales conversions, but it will reward you in many other multidimensional ways - such as friendships, connections and collaborations.

These are worth way more in the grand scheme of things than a thousand followers and likes on your posts.

I saw a meme just this week that said *"Being famous on Instagram is basically the same thing as being rich in Monopoly"* via @rosa_palermo_wellness

It doesn't really mean anything, unless it means something.

Social Media for a New Age labels success as creating a platform you enjoy, a community that you cultivate and interact with lovingly, having a creative outlet, a practice that supports you in many different ways… It really is THE place right now to connect you, your business and your mission with others globally, at the tap of a button.

What I share in this book is to help you remain true to yourself and to your dreams, to enjoy using social media as a tool and creative practice that supports you in making those dreams happen and/or come into fruition.

Simple strategies that are authentic and true,

Passionate, real, in alignment with YOU.

Tune into yourself to remember…

*We can use social media to **ignite our dreams**
on many different levels.
By sharing our gifts and inspiring others.
By serving and supporting each other,
ourselves and the planet.
In co-creating new paradigms.
In bridging dimensions.*

When we show up from that place…
Magic happens.

TIME AND SPACE DISSOLVES IN THE DIGITAL DIMENSION

Words, ideas, downloads, moments, adventures, energy, passion and creativity existing digitally across time and space, all connecting to real people, to each other.**

**We do tend to lose sight or forget that it's actual people on each side of our devices at times!

I bear witness to magic being woven day and night by communities coming together online. Having spent the last couple of years travelling and working online, communicating with my friends, family, clients and community spanning the globe and time-zones, I am so very grateful to be able to connect with them every day through my devices and through social media.

There are many different ways to use this phenomenal technology, and this book is my perspective (which by the way is *"personal, subjective and unique"*).

I've had social media pulsing through my veins since I was a teenager. I remember in the mid-90's, just as networked computers were emerging, I would queue up at lunchtime to use the computer room just to talk to my friends on the other computers in the same room! Twenty years later, multiply that by circa two billion people doing the same globally.

We are using it for our businesses, our social lives and pretty much everything in-between. So, in order to help us use social media more effectively as we transition into a new age, I'll be talking about how to get out of the *social media vortex of doom,* whilst sharing what I know about algorithms. I'll invite you to explore your *social media ego and your social media soul,* giving you simple strategies I use with my 1-2-1 clients on how to tap into your creativity and create consistency with a *framework to flow within.* We'll discuss what it means to be authentic and vulnerable online, different marketing techniques and the power of community for the new paradigm.

Yes, this book is spiritual, emotional, geeky and practical all at the same time!

I hope my words in this book and everything that it provokes in you serve you. I would love to hear from you as you read, please join me on Instagram @katiekdot_socialmediaangel, facebook.com/socialmediaangel, or by using the hashtag #socialmediaforanewage to share with me your ideas, insights, your aha's, and your stories.

You can also share your thoughts and ideas with me in a new closed Facebook Group community I am creating for readers of the book facebook. com/groups/socialmediaforanewage, where you will also get access to exclusive content and online events. Hope to see you there.

Love Kdot x

Chapter One

THE SOCIAL MEDIA VORTEX OF DOOM.

When you feel anxious,
overwhelmed and stressed out,
When it's too much to handle,
When you want to hide, not hang out.
You have entered the
'social media vortex of doom',
Where nothing works
and nothing blooms.
So take a break,
Put your phone down,
Switch airplane mode on,
Relax and chill out.

Entering the Social Media Vortex of Doom

I recently did an online masterclass for a group of authors where I asked; *"How does social media make you feel?"*

'Overwhelm' is what came through for more than half of them. And I hear this a lot from my clients and community that they feel overwhelmed by social media too.

SOCIAL MEDIA
IS A LOT

It's a digital world, a sprawling metropolis, that keeps changing and growing. New highways are built and roads are re-routed, new suburbs pop up in the form of features and updates… Then there are all the people, the adverts and videos that show up in our timelines through sponsored posts and ads. Knocking on our digital doors everyday often unannounced or uninvited, is like having the double-glazing sales men, a Jehovah's witness, plus all of the marketing and sales leaflets dropping through your letterbox and knocking at your door all at the same time.

Woooaaah there. Back off, people!

Then we have our friends, our contemporaries and colleagues posting about what they're up to and with whom, and we then consciously and unconsciously compare ourselves to it all.

There is a lot going on and lots of opportunity to feel overwhelmed daily. Someone told me recently that it makes her feel like her *"neurons are on fire"*.

For those of us who are trying to grow a social media following for our businesses and to support our dreams, there is also another deeper layer of overwhelm and frustration that can come into play.

Social media appears to work like a dream *on the surface* for many, with people seemingly building large audiences on pages and groups overnight, driving sales and making thousands nay millions of $£... But for those of us on the other side of that *'reality'* it can feel very different. It feels disappointing and frustrating and often leads to feelings of lack and feelings of *"not good enough"*.

THIS CREATES A NEGATIVE SPIRAL, A VORTEX. THE SOCIAL MEDIA VORTEX OF DOOM

A high volume of brands and *public figures* are using trained copy writers and marketing techniques which are specifically designed to drive lots of clicks, build email lists, sell products and lifestyles. These many tried and tested ways that create *'engagement'* are being used by many industries on social media, including the mind body spirit and self-development industry.

I'll go into this in more detail later.

There is a sea change happening, particularly among a more conscious, aware and awakening audience, who are bored with this way of doing things. The vibration of these marketing techniques is not in alignment anymore. I read a recent astrology report where the end of the 3D model of marketing on social media within the spiritual community was highlighted…

"The dying, self-deleting old 3D model was to sign up to - or even offer yourself – a program promising a secret or another way to "improve" yourself with an accompanying book, download,

podcasts and private Facebook group. All centred around whoever was offering it/selling it. A sort of "look how enlightened I am/I know something you don't" hard sell, based on the lie that you are flawed or missing something that will turn your life around. It's just glamorous psychic fairy dust to make you feel special, back on track, about to drop the chaos of "ordinary" life for a glorious fresh new start. Isn't all this now feeling outdated, cynical and, worse, an expensive distraction from trusting your own unique process of evolution?
- Lorna Bevan - Hare of the Moon Astrology Facebook Page

Part of the **overwhelm** people suffer from is thinking they have to do it a certain way, that they have to create and manage multiple platforms, content types and products as the only route to success. Thus, we ignore the many other great ways to market yourself online, with one of these ways being content, conversation and community.

The **most simple thing**, to me, is to share your truth, rather than having to make something up. To let your social media feeds be a reflection of what you are doing and who you are in real life, to share the things you are sharing in the real world, with real people!

Social Media is a beautiful bridge (a big rainbow bridge with unicorns trotting across - in my mind!) from the physical dimension to the digital dimension.

Using social media **as the tool** to share your essence, your gifts, your creations, services and products – and connect YOU with a wider community, online and offline.

If you can find ways to share your knowledge, wisdom, skills and service authentically and honestly, then it comes down to you and how others respond to and interact with you.

This can be hard as some people don't know really know what their truth or what their true essence is yet. Layers of conditioning, of ego, masks, fear, hiding… Of thinking we 'should' be this or that…

Showing up on social media really calls on us to get clear with who we are, what our message is and what our values are, and value is, in order to show up fully in our authenticity and integrity.

Recognising your own Social Media Vortex of Doom

Facebooks core newsfeed values of **"personal, subjective and unique"** mean that everyone is having a totally unique experience of social media.

For me, to do social media, life, anything really successfully, you do actually have to show up - and you do it as YOU. I just saw a comment on one of my Instagram posts about this saying *"it takes so much more effort not to be you than be you"* and I completely agree.

Social media can suck the life force out of us… It can, and does, send people spiralling into negative feelings and emotions. It is powerful, way more powerful at doing this than we often give it credit for. How many times have you pulled out your phone, unconsciously tapped on a social network and seen a post that catches you off guard, that changes your mood?

Having an awareness of this really helps.

Also knowing that it takes time, energy, patience and confidence to use social media as a platform for our business helps too… It can help us come out the other side of any negative feelings and emotions that our impatience is creating within us.

Recognising that if you didn't grow up using social media, it can feel even more challenging and not beating yourself up about that. Because not being good at social media can become another stick to beat ourselves with.

It is a totally different kettle of fish for the younger generations, especially the ones that grew up with social media. They have a TOTALLY DIFFERENT experience and relationship to the technology and to the concept of being on social media as a whole. It is such a natural thing for them. When and where you grew up during the evolution of the age of the social media makes a big difference to how you relate to it, and how you use it.

Added to the layers of this anxiety caused by social media - much like watching the mainstream news can make us feel fearful of the world, social media can easily trigger feelings of self-doubt, create comparison, envy, jealousy, separation, anxiety and depression.

No matter how old you are.

That's another element of the social media vortex of doom that we need to navigate while using social media personally and professionally.

I have heard that this is worse for the younger generations, the millennials, especially ones with lots of followers on platforms like Instagram & YouTube. They feel even deeper levels of anxiety than anyone, other than perhaps celebrities - same pressure in some ways, as they feel they have to look a certain way - be it their bodies or their lifestyle.

It is a lot of PRESSURE.

For everyone.

It is keeping up with the Jones' x a million.

I think that if at any point it starts to make you;
More unhappy than happy…
More alone than connected…
More anxious than supported…
Put it down and take a BREAK!

COSMIC CONNECTEDNESS
OVER TECH ADDICTION

Danielle la Porte

Getting out of the Social Media Vortex of Doom.

Take a social media detox.
Switch your phone onto airplane mode.
Get out into nature.

It is a social media myth that taking time off from being on social media is going to limit your success. Yes, consistency is a big factor - social media won't work if you don't post anything ever, or consistently, most of the time. Just like you won't get fit or stay fit if you don't exercise. But content creators have been made to feel that they have to be posting brand new content 24/7, seven days a week to have an impact online.

It is simply not true.

Particularly when you already have lots of content available on the web for people to continue to discover, you don't have to keep publishing new stuff all the time.

Quality not quantity.

While writing this book, I did some research on this and took some accounts and content threads offline for a while to see if it could have a positive effect. To see if it breathes new life into things (creatively) and if it improves engagement - because you stop your audience from taking you and your content for granted. More on this later.

Of course, all of it depends where you are at on your social media journey and how engaged your following or audience is and what type of content you create, and how consistent you have been in the past.

Because it is ***personal, subjective and unique*!**

No matter where you are in your social media journey - I think it is always a good idea to take a break and re-think, re-strategise - REST if you have entered the social media vortex of doom.

IF YOU GET TIRED, LEARN TO REST, # NOT QUIT

Banksy

Nothing good will come out of being in that space - most especially if it is annoying you or creating stress and anxiety.

Remembering that social media is a tool to help us **reach the people that matter most.**

The internet will not break if you take some time out to regroup. So please don't keep posting just because you think you SHOULD. Because so many people do and then wonder why it doesn't get positive results.

It is because we can feel those posts.

Your energy is infused into your social media activity. We might not be able to see your social media vortex of doom, but we on some level are able to feel it.

INNER UNICORN QUESTION TIME

Am I comparing myself, my platforms or follower numbers to others?

Does being on social media fill up my heart or fill me with fear??

Do I have healthy boundaries with social media; am I able to switch it off?

Chapter Two

ACTUALLY, WTF IS AN ALGORITHM?

We love to blame the algorithm,
for everything under the sun,
"My content didn't get seen you know,
Those pesky algorithms are scum!"
But they do have our best interests at heart,
Zuckerberg wants his AI to learn from us
and be smart,
With engagement and community
making it go off the charts.
Getting the stories that matter to us most,
making sure spam and fake news are toast.
So next time you cuss and complain,
Say thank you algorithms,
Amen.

I was sat in the garden one afternoon working on a client project when I found myself muttering, *"effin' algorithms"* under my breath. I was hitting a brick wall with the organic reach of some video content and I couldn't understand why.

For those of you who are new to, or not fluent in, 'social media speak', what I mean by 'organic reach' is how many people are actually getting to see the content. How many timelines and newsfeeds the content is reaching naturally, without having to spend money on it, or by boosting or creating a sponsored post or advert.

The algorithms on Facebook and Instagram, which are the two main social media platforms I focus on with my clients (and who I shall refer to as just Facebook from here on in - as they also own and run Instagram), are ever-changing... They are ever-evolving. You think you have it figured out, and bam, they go and change again.

Facebook (and life) are iterative by their very nature. Facebook tell us they are *"1% finished"* and have an iterative strategy. That strategy is: *"to keep improving through ongoing testing and feedback."*

Since I started writing this book, Facebook announced more big changes to the algorithm... And although there is a lot of noise and complaining (always) about these changes and what it will do to the 'reach' of the content, the truth is they are an extension, an evolution, an iteration of the changes they had already begun to make.

A lot of us using social media think we know what we are talking about when we talk about this "algorithm" and people often blame things not going well on social media on the 'algorithm' - but do we **really** know or understand what it is?

I say 'we' because I have to keep educating myself as to what it actually does VS what I 'think' it does. I try to always find out for myself rather than rely on what the so-called experts say. How the algorithm works for one person, is going to be different to how it works for someone else, because it is **"personal, subjective and unique."**

*"Our success is built on getting people the stories that matter to them most. If you could look through thousands of stories every day and choose the 10 that were most important to you, which would they be? The answer should be your News Feed. It is **personal, subjective and unique** – and defines the spirit of what we hope to achieve."*
- Facebook Press Room June 2016.

In its very basic form, an algorithm is a set of instructions given to a computer to solve a specific problem. An algorithm is a formula; it is computer code. In the case of Facebook, they have many, many algorithms all working together to solve lots of "problems", which for them is to process the huge amounts of posts, data and actions taking place on their platforms every day and how to sort those out.

A few of the things the Facebook algorithms want to do, according to their blurb' is…

Getting the posts you want to see the most to the top of your newsfeed.

It is learning from us and is working to predict what you want to see based on your previous actions e.g. whether you liked something, someone or left a comment.

Artificial intelligence is also involved, as it is with many things these days and I'm still getting my head around exactly how AI fits together with the algorithms on Facebook and Instagram. The concept of Artificial Intelligence can be a bit scary not only due to the amount of data constantly being collected, but how that is being used and what it actually means… You may have read that machines could take over the world one day… Which is an interesting idea to consider, especially with recent reports in the news about military drones which will no longer be controlled by humans but instead by AI, which will choose which targets to kill.

This is truth about what is happening on planet earth right now, killer drones controlled by artificial intelligence.

We need to recognise that AI - artificial intelligence - is becoming more and more integrated into our lives, as we become more integrated with technology…

Whether we know about it or not.

The most obvious versions of AI at work that I am aware of are the digital assistants such as Apple's Siri… Alexa on Amazon's Echo… and Facebook's yet to be released assistant, which Mark Zuckerberg has been building…

"I've built a simple AI that can talk to my phone and computer, that can control my home, including lights, temperature, appliances, music and security, that learns my tastes and patterns, that can learn new words and concepts, and that can even entertain Max. It uses several artificial intelligence techniques, including natural language processing, speech recognition, face recognition, and reinforcement learning…"
- Mark Zuckerberg *facebook.com*

Right now, though, the AI (the commercial AI we see anyway!) is a still a little bit clumsy. It doesn't understand the complexities of how a human thinks or feels... It wants to understand, or we want it to understand...

A super brain in Silicon Valley, Professor Hinton, known as the "godfather of AI", is a pioneer of something called machine learning. This deep learning enables computers to create programmes that solve problems themselves - mimicking the neural networks. It is actually modelled on how human toddlers learn.

Google also announced recently that their new AI assistant will be able to call and book appointments, sounding like a human, even 'umming and erring' in the right places, and that it is so convincing people won't know if they are talking to a human or talking to a computer.

From what I understand on social media, the AI we encounter when it comes to the content in our timelines, is learning what you like, *by* what you like... And then it is predicting what you would like to see, sorting your posts into the order it thinks you want to see them in, with the most important at the top. But for most people, it isn't really getting that right yet.

Facebook knows what makes you happy, sad, angry or wow'd, by the emoticons you use. It knows if you like watching videos more than clicking on links, or if you prefer photos and images over plain text.

Facebook now give us tools to create short text updates that look prettier by allowing us to add colour and images to our words? They have given us stickers and gifs to use in the comments. That is because they have learnt that generally we respond more when there is a visual aspect to content and communication. This is why MEME's became so popular. Words on a coloured background or a nice image will often get a higher engagement than a simple text update.

I can pay testament to that. When I started working on best-selling author Diana Coopers' Facebook page five years ago - before memes were a *thing* - we took her plain text status updates and turned them into graphics. It resulted in her page growing from 20,000 to 100,000 in about six months - because they were more eye catching and people like to share them. Memes were one of the most popular content types for a good few years, although their popularity is on the wane due to the sheer volume of them now on social media.

Facebook not only know that we like pretty things. They know what events in the world heighten and effect our emotions... From elections, to big sports games, to terror attacks... They have even been known to see if they can control our emotions directly by what we see in our newsfeed.

Legal? Apparently so... Ethical? Not so much...

In January 2012, Facebook conducted secret experiments to see if they could manipulate our moods with the content we saw in our timelines. Facebook engineers changed the content being seen, by using an algorithm, in the newsfeed for nearly 700,000 people. Some people were shown content with happy and positive words; some were shown negative and upsetting content. They then watched to see if these 'users' were more likely to post either positive or negative things themselves. If you google 'Facebook experiment to control emotions', you will see a number of articles in the mainstream media from 2014 about it.

It can boggle the mind (and be a bit unsettling) when you think about the power that Facebook and other big tech companies (Google, Apple etc.) have through their access to our data and how they are monitoring us or how they could also be manipulating us.

NB. Since I wrote these words the Cambridge Analytica/Facebook data scandal has come to light.

Especially when we are spending more time online than ever.

According to recent stats I have seen that the amount of time we spend online equates to about four hours a day for a lot of people and that we check our phones around 150 times per day!!! But that is a bigger topic for another chapter (or probably another book!)

Let's go back to understanding more about what the algorithm is actually doing in the background and with content.

When Facebook are promoting their products or features then they will usually give that function more chance to be seen by allowing that kind of content to reach further.

E.G. Facebook Live

What I often say is that, *"the gates of the algorithm are open"*, when a new feature or product is launched.

Facebook want LIVE to be successful, for it to perform well so that lots of people use it. They note that Facebook Live gets x6 more engagement than normal video and promotes...

ACTIVE ENGAGEMENT
OVER PASSIVE VIEWING.

In one of the more recent updates from Mark Zuckerberg (January 12th 2018), he talks about how research with Universities in the USA show that active engagement with people we know, like and love, creates more happiness and well-being than passive scrolling of content from brands and publishers.

Facebook's mission, according to Mark Zuckerberg, is to..

HELP CONNECT EVERYONE
AROUND THE WORLD
AND BRING THE WORLD
CLOSER TOGETHER.

Facebook

Across the many Facebook pages I have admin access to through my work, I see that Facebook Live **will** reach the furthest. Uploading a pre-recorded video directly to Facebook **will** reach much further than posting a YouTube or Vimeo link (unless it gets a lot of engagement quickly).

I could get super geeky about this with you and share how video gets more engagement than links – basically, it's due to the size of the visual and the instant play feature (we love a moving image!), because it captures our attention more, and therefore we respond in a more emotive way, which in turn tells the algorithm and Facebook we like it, so they show us more of it.

Get it? Got it? Good :)

It is also good to remember that Facebook want to be the number one platform for video, and other platforms such as YouTube and Vimeo, are therefore in competition with them. I assume this is why videos uploaded directly to Facebook have a more attractive placing on the platform. It makes sense to me that those uploaded directly look better and thus perform better than a link to your video on another (competitive) platform.

A similar thing has been happening recently with their new 'Instant Articles' feature - it is a relatively new native feature for blog posts, which coincides with their announcement to limit reach for slow loading websites. Instant articles are a speedier way of articles loading within Facebook. They want to keep everyone and all the content in the platform rather than leading them away.

"Fast and Responsive. Leveraging the same technology used to display photos and videos quickly in the Facebook app, articles load instantly in News Feed, and readers really like the speed. 10X Faster than standard mobile web articles. 20% More Instant Articles read on average. 70% Less Likely to Abandon the Article." instantarticles.fb.com

It's worth exploring if you are a blogger and you publish a lot of links to your articles. This could be a better way to create higher organic reach for your written/blog content. As an aside to this - I have been using the approach of publishing blogs in full, as text with an image, instead of with links, as these tend to get a higher reach too.

I am all about building relationships through content, not just about driving clicks or sign ups. It makes sense to me that not asking someone to leave something they are already reading to click away, or sign up to something before being able to finish, means you limit the chance of someone seeing something you have spent time and energy creating. Therefore, you decrease the chance of building a relationship with that person over time, particularly if you are still trying to establish yourself on social media.

I must admit I often eye roll when someone tells me I have to click through to their blog to read more, particularly on Instagram where there is no clickable link in the text. Let me read it right there! It also works for you in terms of the algorithm, as you are more likely to get someone to like or comment on something that they can read or watch in full on the platform.

I ALWAYS encourage everyone to test these things for themselves and to use the tools and features that suit them and their audience best, rather than do it just because of the algorithm or just because an "expert" tells you to do it, or I tell you do it.

Because really anything is possible, depending on what you do and how your audience respond to you.

Personal, subjective and unique.

There is an awesome astrologer called Kaypacha who does a weekly YouTube video called the Pele Report and he (or his team) post this YouTube link to his Facebook page. He doesn't upload directly on Facebook, so he is in some ways going against what I would consider "best practice". However, his YouTube videos are **really popular** and get shared a lot on Facebook. I saw a recent one that had 75,000+ views in a just a few days, so it doesn't matter that he posts a link to YouTube on Facebook, as his fans and community just want to watch his videos - and they are happy to click through to YouTube because they have a relationship with him and with his content, because it means something to them.

That is something really important to remember.

The ever-changing, ever-evolving, ever-iterating algorithm may affect you if you are posting lots of links, lots of spam and asking people to click, like and share - or if you are posting content that is not getting any kind of connection or engagement.

If that is the case it is probably time to revise your social media strategy. If people care about and want your content, then the algorithm is working for you not against you.

Facebook tell us that they want to create *"opportunities to interact with the people you care about"*, the *"people that matter most"*, and that this is what they are working towards with the recent algorithm changes. We should listen to them and create a social media strategy that creates opportunities to interact with the people we know and care about, to the people that matter most. Authentic communication is where the gates to the algorithm portal are open.

And I loved this comment I saw about the recent changes; to me it kind of sums things up…

"Not even mad about this update. The only people who should be scared are spammers, bot-lovers, and "me-me-me-marketers". If you post actionable, helpful content and generously provide value to your fans, you have nothing to worry about--except maybe a little less competition from the shady marketers. The Facebook-ocalypse terror (17th one if I count correctly) is just thrashing over nothing." Alexa on Facebook via Buffer.com Blog.

INNER UNICORN QUESTION TIME

How can I make my content conversational and engaging?

How can I be 'personal, subjective and unique' with my strategy?

What does being iterative mean for me?

Chapter 3

SOCIAL MEDIA EGO VS SOCIAL MEDIA SOUL

Likes feel good, follows and comments too,
Nothing wrong with that,
until it becomes all that we pursue.
It can affect our value,
but is it true?
There is nothing to do,
just be you.

As a teen, I wanted to be famous when I grew up. A lot of us probably did, it was the thing to aspire to, especially with all the big TV talent shows of the time like Pop Idol and beyond, which promised to make 'ordinary folk' famous. It has taken me a while to dissolve the heavy conditioning I have towards celebrity culture and I am still shaking it off now.

But being famous is something many of us still aspire to, except now it's different... Being YouTube or Instagram famous, rather than on the TV has become much more accessible and is a big business if you are an 'influencer'...

Being a social media influencer is a career path in our digital age, with many looking to build big social media followings, hits and clicks to blogs and YouTube channels, in order to make money from brands and businesses who want to advertise and market their products to their burgeoning audiences. It is a booming industry but is it a good one?

And has it already gotten out of control?

It plays very much to our social media ego, focusing on follower numbers and celebrity status. It has the power to place the ego in control and to let it get out of control. It's often about beauty, status, power, wealth and appearing to 'have it all'. I've heard stories of fashion influencers who are now more powerful than the fashion houses, designers or models themselves, charging vast amounts of money and having a long list of demands to feature products and people in their social media feeds.

When thinking about being or becoming an influencer, what comes to your mind?

HOW CAN WE BE INFLUENCERS WITH OUR SOCIAL MEDIA SOUL RATHER THAN OUR SOCIAL MEDIA EGO?

What is a Social Media Influencer for a New Age?

For me it would be someone using their platform to help people, using their influence to effect positive change for their community, as well as for the masses and being rewarded for that in many different ways; financially, emotionally and spiritually.

Less exclusivity and more accessibility, also means that many of us who are present on social media are getting a taste of 'fame' ourselves. I have met people that I have only known online and felt a little star struck. I know people have done the same with me and even more so with my clients and friends who have big social media followings.

Just this week I was walking down Glastonbury High Street when I saw someone do a double take, come up to me and say *"Hi!! Katie??! It's Margaret-Anne - from Instagram!"*

Which is both awesome and weird all at the same time.

Wanting to become social media famous in this day and age is as natural for us now, as wanting to be TV famous was when I was a teenager.

"Neuroscience and attachment theory offer an explanation of what we are looking for: according to recent research, normal human development requires that we feel recognised and seen by others."
- Psychology Today

But because of this when we get on social media, there is a tendency for us to act differently because of our need for recognition. I also think that when we see ourselves on a screen, in the same way that we used to see people through the lens of the TV or movies screen, it activates this part of us.

As my publisher Sean Patrick said when we met to discuss this book, *'we are not all Beyoncé!'* Social media plays to that part of our ego which makes us think we *have* to be Beyoncé. (Not that there is anything wrong with being a little bit Beyoncé!! But lets' get a reality check here).

EGO: I: a person's sense of self-esteem or self-importance.

Our ego is having a FREAKIN' field day when it comes to social media. Social Media for a New Age is in part about recognising when our social media ego is getting out of control and how to shift it into a better balance and connect with our social media soul.

My **social media ego** - wants big follower numbers, doesn't even really care who the followers are; she wants to look and feel popular, successful, important and in control.

My **social media soul,** on the other hand, really wants community, connection, engagement with like-minded people, to make friends she can get to know, meet clients she can support and serve with her knowledge and skills.

I would love you to acknowledge and say hi now to your social media ego and your social media soul, because they will both play a part in your social media journey. When we bear witness to both sides - it makes it so much easier to get back into balance when we are leaning too much into the ego.

Every time I post, I have to check in with myself on this. Because the sweet rush of likes and comments? *Ahhhhh, makes you feel goooood, doesn't it?*

My **social media ego** loooooooves getting lots of 'likes' on posts, and it likes those 'likes' to come through fast. I have noticed I have a tendency to keep checking and checking again to see if there are any new likes, comments, hearts immediately after posting... I know that I am not alone in this.

"Researchers have confirmed that the desire to be 'Liked' on Facebook is a universal phenomenon. We all want to feel worthy of love and belonging. In some ways, the 'Likes' we get on Facebook satisfies this need in a distorted way."
- Psychology Today

My **social media soul** however is happy to let a post go out into the ether and do its thing. Trusting that it will be seen by the people it needs to be seen by, without the need for validation. My social media soul, she doesn't NEED the likes and comments, although she welcomes, feels and receives the love and comments gracefully whenever they appear.

But it isn't just followers and likes… Comparison is another big one for our **social media ego.**

I checked in on Lucy Sheridan's Instagram account about this topic. Lucy is known as The Comparison Coach and I actually found her outing her own social media ego. High fives to that, Lucy. It's really good to know that we are not alone. It helps us all when we share, and are aware to, how comparison can create mayhem in our thinking, and can hinder our enjoyment of being on social media.

"Outing my ego! My comparison has been back with a vengeance this week and I have been really beating myself up about my Instagram - not being interesting enough, funny enough, helpful enough, not being as far along as other people and their profile following. It sounds ridiculous when I read this back to myself but hey it has hurt - or rather I have hurt myself. Well NO MORE! I'm going back to my own lane to tend my grass and its greenery. I love hanging out here and I won't let my Comparison ruin it. Can you relate? Does IG sometimes fuel your self-confidence wobbles? I've got you xxx"
- @LucySheridan

Notice that she checks in with her **social media soul** here too, *"I love hanging out here and I won't let my comparison ruin it."*

Mel Wells, author of the *Goddess Revolution* (who's room I rented when I was in Bali), has a big social media following. She has been speaking out about this ego vs soul trap on social media too…

"Social media… We all use it… But what are we really using it for? Is it adding to our lives or taking away…? Is it bringing us closer together or pushing us further apart…? Where is it actually leading us? And if it IS having a negative effect on our beautiful minds, what can we do about it?" @Iammelwells

Mel and Lucy are good examples of women with a great platform, who struggle with social media anxiety too. You are not alone in struggling with social media anxiety and it is SO important that we talk about it openly and share about it with each other so that we can help to heal it individually and collectively.

I think that most of us who are active social media users at some point suffer from some form of social media related anxiety, and some of us on a daily basis without even realising it. If you do it, it's something to learn to recognise, take a closer look at and get help with, if it gets out of control, and to take a break away from social media to regain control.

If we are feeling lost, afraid, if we are in our *social media vortex of doom* then yes, we can loose the sense of connection and belonging - let's be honest, who hasn't had days where you hate everyone and everything you see on social media… Including your friends!

When we are feeling great, when we are in our **social media soul**, it can bring us closer together, it helps us to cultivate connection and a sense of belonging. But equally when we feel hurt, lost, in pain or out of control with our lives it can feel like the complete opposite - all the picture-perfect moments captured and shared, that affect us quite deeply.

It depends on **where we are at,** in each given moment.

It depends on what emotional state we are in, when we are on the platform. And this can make it hard to navigate the space especially when we are wanting to use social media as a tool for our business - the lines get oh so blurry.

If you feel your ego out of control or you are lost in the vortex of doom then taking time out to meditate, to connect back in with yourself is an important part of a healthy social media practice.

I want to share this extract from the *Goddess is Speaking* blog, by my friend and client Karen Ruimy, which really helps me when I want to connect in with my soul.

"When you connect with your soul and live life from the awareness this brings, you will be living on a higher energetic level. You will attract the greater brilliance of higher energies into your life. You will grow to understand the gifts that your soul has to offer which are the tools for you to create the life that you dream of. Last but not least you will align yourself to the rhythm of the flow of life because the energy of the soul resonates with that. You will experience the sense of being in harmony with a higher order and living with coincidences, good surprises and doors opening before you. Or if they shut you'll know it's to show you the value of change.

Enjoy the journey!"
- @karenruimy

Managing the dance between the soul and the ego with social media (and life) becomes a real practice of conscious awareness.

INNER UNICORN QUESTION TIME

Am I posting from a place of love or fear?

Am I trying to impress or impact?

Am I seeking or needing approval and/or attention from others?

Chapter 4

YOUR VIBE ATTRACTS YOUR TRIBE

When we show up and shine,
sharing our essence, our vibe,
The ones we attract are our friends,
and are our tribe.
No need to search,
so far and so wide.
Let your energy align,
Bringing the right ones
to your timeline.

'Your Vibe Attracts Your Tribe' is a phrase I used to use a lot in relation to growing your audience on social media. I saw that the energy, *Your Vibe*, the essence that you share and communicate through your content, is felt by others and attracts the right-for-you kind of people to connect, be it followers, clients or friends.

"Vibe: a person's emotional state or the atmosphere of a place as communicated to and felt by others."

- Google Dictionary

I actually registered the UK trademark for it, created a book proposal and did a couple of workshops using the concept of your vibe attracts your tribe. People often comment and tell me how it helped them understand being on social media better. It felt important to include a chapter on it, although my relationship to the phrase has shifted a lot in recent times.

Why? I read something which suggested it was offensive to indigenous tribes to use the term. And because it started to get used in reference to just about everything, to the point where it started to lose its meaning and be misunderstood in the context I was using it. Have you noticed that? That when a thing get adopted and used a lot, its context can become different and confusing? So, I fell out of love with the word for describing our social media followings, community, audience, family... In its over use, and its misuse, it lost its essence... it lost its vibe...

"Tribe: a social division in a traditional society consisting of families or communities linked by social, economic, religious, or blood ties, with a common culture and dialect, typically having a recognised leader"
- Google Dictionary

Connecting to each other to "communities with a common culture" is human nature.

I am going to take us back in time... Way, way back to 1999 when the internet was just a baby, and social media as such didn't exist.

It was in my final year at university, in 6YBF... (Years Before Facebook), when some of my university friends heard that some students at another University had just sold a website for a cool million £. There were five of us; a software engineer, a creative genius, his graphic designer brother, a law student and me, and we created a platform, a website called 'Leeds Graduate', aimed at students graduating from our university, as we would be doing that summer. It was in fact a social network, and we were in talks with some big companies to create an international hub for graduates all around the world.

'Friends Forever - Don't lose touch' was our strap-line.

However, the dot com bubble of that era crashed during the year 2000, we had also been a bit too early with the idea for it to take hold. We didn't even have WIFI at that point in time, let alone 4G. When I went to see the movie "The Social Network" based on the Facebook story a decade or more later, some of the similarities were a bit close for comfort. Funny to think I might have been a billionaire in a parallel life!

The reason for sharing this story is that I have always seen these platforms, this technology, this tool we have been gifted, as a way for us to connect or keep connecting with people we know or want to know.

That is the tribal part. It was the reason we created Leeds Graduate and it's at the crux of 'social networking'. It's a human part.

Community. And what a wonderful part it is.

That is the magic and that is the essence of Your Vibe Attracts Your Tribe. It is what Facebook is trying do, it is trying to get back on mission.

BRINGING PEOPLE CLOSER TOGETHER

Facebook

In November 2014, I went on my first big overseas solo adventure to Nepal. I travelled to a family-run retreat centre at the foot of the Himalayas. I subsequently connected on Facebook with a few of the teachers and guides there. Forward-wind 3 years and I am in Bali, when Bipin, my meditation teacher who is living in Kathmandu, pops up in a Facebook comment and asks me if I want to jump on a Facebook Live chat with him about mindfulness! So, next thing I know, I'm in a Facebook group with people from all over the world, streaming live a conversation between Bali and Nepal!

We get so caught up in the frustrations of thinking we need hundreds of thousands or millions of followers in our tribes, and we forget how wonderful it is that we can connect to one person, three people, ten people, one hundred people, no matter where they are!

How we connect and with whom we connect to changes over time. Our vibe changes and so does our tribe. When we all joined Facebook ten years or so ago, our lives, and even how we related to social media were all very different.

When Facebook took off in 2007, I was working in the music industry and I was spending a lot of time going out partying and clubbing... ten years later, I'm working in a completely different industry and I spend my time at workshops, in cosy cafes and restaurants (or staying home having a salt bath and watching Netflix...). I have changed a lot over the past decade and where I hang out and with who, has changed too.

So, *your vibe attracts your tribe* is also an invitation to choose where and with whom you hang out with in the great Social Media Metropolis. Just like in life we broaden our horizons, we move house, we meet new people, you can do the same on social media.

You get to choose. And many of us don't, we stay stuck. Your experience of social media can shift from a negative one to a positive one in the act of choosing.

In a masterclass I gave recently one of the things that people didn't like about social media was the negative talk and aggression they witnessed online. There is a lot of chatter online, that's a FACT. That isn't going to go away anytime soon, so it is up to you to tell the platforms what and who YOU do and don't like. Then they will stop showing up in your newsfeed.

Just like you might stick on your letterbox… **No junk mail please.** If you click the top right hand of a post, you will see that you have an option to hide something or someone. You can mute people for thirty days. You can unfollow them. If what you see is upsetting you in any way - then perhaps it is time to start changing up your social media feed.

One of my favourite people in the whole world, author and creator of magic Lisa Lister @sassylisalister, tells us in her book '*Witch'* to;

CALL BACK
OUR POWER NOW

Lisa Lister

If you wouldn't want to hang out with someone in real life, why hang out with them online? It can be perceived as a social faux pas to unfriend or unfollow in case someone sees and you upset them. You can't make the age-old excuse of *"I'm errr… washing my hair"* to get out of meeting up. But let's get real here, would you really notice with all the noise online now if someone has unfollowed YOU? And would you take offence if they did?

There is no alert or unfollow police. So, what really happens when you unfollow someone? Nothing. Your timeline becomes a place that lights you up and doesn't drag you down. That's what happens!

You are letting people energetically into your space when you let them into your timelines. We need to protect our space and our energy, it is vital in these current times. Just as you might sage your house or protect your energy with a bubble of light when you go out into the world… Look at how you can adapt some these same practices and principles online as you have offline.

Author of *'Earth is Hiring'*, @PetaJean spoke about creating discipline with her Instagram community, I love what she shares in relation to this;

"Last week I started practising more discipline with social media - going from 'checking whenever I felt like it' to being on insta 1 times a day, 30 mins. My soul was so clear 'gf you cannot go where you need to go now with that much information and diverse AF frequencies penetrating you field throughout the day'. Duh."

BE EXACTLY WHO YOU SAY YOU ARE.

We do have this tendency to behave differently online to offline, but it is still us… Our thought forms, our energy converted into the written word, our moments, our photos, our voices… Why do we think we have to behave differently? Or that we can behave differently?

IT IS US.
ALL OF IT.

For anyone that has been on the receiving end of a nasty comment or post or has simply witnessed people trolling - you have to wonder what is going on for the person on the other side of that. We can have compassion, but we can **also block them.** We do not want that kind of energy messing up our vibe or being in our tribe.

"Every thought we think is creating our future."
- Louise Hay.

Every thought, every post, every comment, everything.

Our vibe attracts our tribe and it attracts our LIFE.

It is we, the humans (I don't think it was aliens… but that could be a whole other conversation!), that have built and created these platforms. We are the ones that use them every day for hours and hours - not always consciously or productively, mind you, but we *are* the ones that are using them.

It's human nature. And how we show up on social media *is* human nature, in all its wild and wonderful forms and variations.

So, we have to be discerning.

We can choose to use the platforms to connect with real people, to reach out with content that is creative, positive, informative, helpful and healing, that is in service to the world at large. We can use it to connect with people in a way that has never been possible before.

IT IS UP TO US
TO CHOOSE
HOW WE USE IT.

Just after I had got back to London from Bali, in a local residents' community Facebook group I'm in, someone I know posted about a young Balinese man who had just been seriously injured in a motorbike accident. They were with him at the scene of the crash and went with him to hospital. It was going to cost $10,000 dollars for life saving surgery, without which the hospital wouldn't operate and he would die. Within forty-eight hours we had raised enough money through the group, for a complete stranger. Everyone pulling together and donating.

It saved his life and it would not have happened without that Facebook Group.

How AMAZING, inspiring and thought provoking is that?!

How many more lives can we save? Maybe the story you share with your community online will change someone's life… Save someone's life.

We are super quick to social media bash. To get annoyed. To be all in the Yin and forget about the Yang. To fall & dive into the social media vortex of doom, to get all up into our social media ego rather than listening to our social media soul.

There is so much good that can be achieved through social media and people are using it for good causes. I just saw one of my old friends Nicki @andtheywentwild in London posting about her local primary school, which is being threatened for closure in the next seven days. She is rallying her local community through Facebook and now has set up an Avaaz online petition to collect signatures. She has taken things into her own hands by adopting social media as the tool to help her and I hope the power of social media and her community save their school.

Organisations like Avaaz, *"the campaigning community, bringing people-powered politics to decision making worldwide,"* are using social media to affect change. There was an article in Guardian which asked *"can online activism really change the world?"* Avaaz means 'voice' and it has over thirty million members worldwide, running big and small campaigns, working to, *"try to unlock the secrets of the internet – of what makes one video of a cute kitten falling over go viral, but not another – and to bring those skills to bear not on Justin Bieber's career or Lady Gaga's album sales, but potential genocide, forced rape, species extinction."*

Powerful stuff and real examples of social media being used for good.

Some of the big named authors in my sphere of awareness who are using their platform for the greater good is Elizabeth Gilbert, Brene Brown, Cheryl Strayed, Glennon Dolye Melton, Marie Forleo and co. with the Compassion Collective, a charity they set up in response to the Syrian refugee crisis.

"Please, take hold of your power today by using your voice and platform for good. Courage and compassion are contagious – people want to be brave, but they need you to be brave first. Join us as a Compassion Collective Organizer by telling your world: I STAND WITH LOVE. "
http://thecompassioncollective.org

Let's take a moment now to tune out the noise, the bullshit, the selfies and the sales copy, and really appreciate the good that social media is and what WE can do with it.

Take three deep breathes and give gratitude for all the good that social media is doing and has done in the world.

THE POWER
OF THE TRIBE

Last year, best-selling Hay House author, Diana Cooper got sick. Diana has been my client for about five years now, and I manage her Facebook page. After a big operation, Diana got a bad infection and took a turn for the worse. We had been posting to her Facebook page what was happening, and Diana's granddaughter was sending me emails with updates to share with everyone. At one point it was looking very serious indeed, so Tim Whild, her co-author, wrote a message asking everyone to send prayers, love and healing.

Diana has a community on social media of over 200,000 people worldwide and the response from them was **phenomenal.** We believe it contributed massively towards her return to good health. She is now more vibrant than ever!

GIVE PEOPLE THE POWER TO BUILD COMMUNITY AND BRING THE WORLD CLOSER TOGETHER

Facebook

Facebook think so. One of their priorities is now Groups. During 2017 they held their first Communities Summit, where Mark Zuckerberg gathered all the biggest group admins and his team together, announcing a new mission for Facebook that will guide their work over the next decade.

"More than 1 billion people around the world use Groups, and more than 100 million people are members of "meaningful groups." These are groups that quickly become the most important part of someone's experience on Facebook. Today we're setting a goal to help 1 billion people join meaningful communities like these."

- Facebook Press Room.

https://newsroom.fb.com/news/2017/06/our-first-communities-summit-and-new-tools-for-group-admins/

Use the tools that social media gives us, be it Facebook Groups, Messenger, Instagram, Twitter, WhatsApp… to create or join meaningful communities.

I have met A LOT of incredible people through social media who are very important and dear to me, from all over the world. You know who you are and I love you!!!!!

Take a moment to think about some of the awesome people you have met and friends you have made - be it through leaving a comment or messaging someone. Through a Facebook group, or by reading a blog. From reaching out to tell someone what they are doing in the world is awesome.

And just look… they are now one of your besties!

That reminds me of a lovely story about one of my dear friends and spiritual superstar Gail Love Schock who had been following me on social media. She saw I was local to her in London from an Instagram post and reached out to literally say, *"you love unicorns, I love unicorns. You are in Chiswick, I am in Chiswick. Fancy a cuppa?"* The rest is history!

There are people I would not have met,
Or have been reunited with.
Kisses I wouldn't have kissed.
Memories I wouldn't have made.
Places I would not have travelled to….

Having my friends, my family, well-wishers, supporters literally **in my pocket,** makes a big difference to me. It has helped me travel to far flung places by myself… It doesn't feel like I am on my own when I can check in, no matter the time or place, see what everyone is up to and share some of my moments, my experiences. That's my TRIBE right there.

For that social media, I thank you.

But it is not like that for everyone. This dropped into my inbox recently and it made me feel sad. One of my community wrote me saying that she, *"wouldn't call it a love hate relationship with social media. More like a hate hate relationship."* Those are pretty strong words.

I'm up for creating **"a love love relationship"** with social media, are you?
Magic happens when you adopt a
strategy of Love.
Love for yourself.
Love for each other.
And for the world.

I am feeling big love for my social media family right now and I hope it helps you to love and appreciate yours. Your true tribe doesn't just live online; you may meet on messenger or in a group or a comment box... But then that will expand and you'll see each other at Workshops, gigs, festivals... On top of Glastonbury Tor... On a beach in Bali... In your backyard... And beyond.

INNER UNICORN QUESTION TIME

What can I do to cultivate a community I care about, that cares about me?

Who have I met, what experiences have I had or what good has happened in my life thanks to social media?

How do I best manage my energy online?

Chapter Five

THE AGE OF SOCIAL MEDIA

It has come so far
in such a short space of time,
Social media has spread quickly,
And created a new paradigm.
From dial up, to WIFI and now 4G,
We are hyper connected
But are we free?
It is up to us now to take this technology,
To use it wisely
and more consciously.

After University, when the start-up didn't work out, I got a job working in the music and broadcast industry. I worked my way up over a couple of years from answering phones at major record labels to becoming PA to one of the hottest Radio 1 DJ's at the time, Dave 'Dance Anthems' Pearce. From there I went to his management company, helping to look after some of the UK's biggest Radio DJs.

Social media was very new at this time, it was pretty much an unknown entity. MySpace appeared first and became the biggest platform around. There were no social media agencies or social media departments, having a digital team, a MySpace account and a decent website was considered pretty cutting edge.

The music industry was burying its head in the sand about the power of digital media. Music file sharing platforms like Napster were banned from being viewed at work, which I always thought was ridiculous. *"If we can't see it, it doesn't exist right?"* How could we know what was actually going on online if we were banned from seeing it? We were actually able to determine how popular a track was going to be in clubland by the amount of times it was being file-shared - but it wasn't good for single sales!

Being part of the mainstream media machine, I also knew how hard it was for people to get on the radio, in the press and on TV without an agent, PR team or record deal.

One of the acts I represented at the time, Firin' Squad, a DJ crew known best for playing garage, R'N'B & Hip Hop, had just lost their national radio show on Kiss FM when I suggested we did this thing called a 'podcast'. I knew these guys had a big audience offline in clubland, plus thousands of fans of the radio show. So, if the radio station wasn't going to broadcast them anymore, we would create our own show and put it out via MySpace.

We met in the studio after hours and recorded it at Wise Buddah, where I worked. The irony that I worked at a place called Wise Buddah is not lost on me now!! And it was a huge success! The listener figures were as big, if not bigger than the radio show itself. One year later, we won Gold in the first ever "Best Internet Programme" category at the Sony Radio Academy Awards. A very proud moment, one of my favourites.

When I look back at how social media was then compared to how it is now… A mere ten years ago… there is simply is no comparison…

It's now mainstream media.
It's alternative media.
It is personal media.

It's publishing.
And PR.

It's marketing.
And market research.
Product development.
And artistic direction.
Advertising.
Brand building.
Sales & Selling.

Blogging & micro blogging.
Podcasting.
Broadcasting.
Live streaming.
Vlogging.
Mind boggling.

It is search & searching.
Reviews & reviewing.
Listening and learning.

Fandom.
And secret stalking.

It is relationship building,
Customer servicing.
It is client relationship managing.
It is community building.

It is online dating.
And friendship making.

I could go on…

And it all started as a place to keep in touch and share things with your friends & family. Memes & cat videos anyone? And now, well now, it is what it is!! It has taken over the business world and our social world.

I wrote a rather prophetic article called "Surfing the Internet" for my school magazine when I was sixteen, where I predicted the rise of social media…

"How far will the internet go? And how long before it not only takes over the business world but the social world as well?"
- Me, 1996

Some pretty spot on pre-cog activity from a sixteen year-old Kdot. (And I also kinda love how my writing style hasn't changed that much. Such.a.geek.)

In light of all this, how can we possibly be expected to know how to do all of the things that being online can do and do them expertly well, under just the title "social media"?

Personally, I find the expectation to be able to do everything that social media experts suggest we do to be successful online is quite overwhelming. Even with my multi- disciplined skill set, there are still so MANY, MANY, MANY aspects and avenues to explore with social media.

I often think, if I worked in Television, say, people wouldn't come to me and expect me to develop a program idea, film it, get it a distribution deal, PR it, grow an audience, get advertisers on board and then sell it. But in social media there is still an expectation that you know how to do it all!

I often go from being a marketing strategist to a business/life coach, to a content producer to tech support all in the space of one client call.

Remembering that we do not have to do it all can really help (it helps me!)

TAKE A BREATH. CREATE SPACE. ASK FOR HELP.

We do not all have to use it in the same way as everyone else.
We do not have to be on all of the platforms.
We do not have to create as much content as we think we do.

Personal, Subjective and Unique.

We all have a different use for it.
We all have a different reason for being on it.
We all have a different understanding of it.
We all have a different expertise or
abilities for it.
We all have different relationships with it.
We will all have different phases with it.

And like I have said before, you get to CHOOSE. Ahhh, how good does that feel?

So many people come to me thinking they have to do it all, and they need to know how to do it all, that they are already behind and have so much catching up to do that it creates a block to getting started, or getting it moving, growing, evolving…

I've been there from the beginning, playing with social media as it has grown up into the adolescent that it is becoming. Some of you will only have just started hanging out with it in the last few years or maybe you've barely been introduced, maybe you have been with hanging out on it on a personal level and now want to start using it for your business...

HONOUR WHERE YOU ARE IN YOUR
SOCIAL MEDIA JOURNEY.

I feel at the moment that we are so bombarded by the sponsored adverts on *'How to make 40k in 4 minutes though Facebook ads'*, *'How to fill your client list in a nano-second using Facebook Groups'*, *et al* that we are losing sight of all of the other wonderful things about social media.

This kind of messaging has created false expectations about how to make money online, about marketing and I think it has spoilt the space. Ahead of his time comedian Bill Hicks, who sadly died in 1994, ten years before Zuckerberg even thought of The Facebook, makes me chuckle in this routine about Marketing;

"By the way if anyone here is in advertising or marketing… kill yourself… No really, there's no rationalisation for what you do and you are Satan's little helpers. Okay – kill yourself – seriously. You are the ruiner of all things good, seriously. No this is not a joke, you're going, "there's going to be a joke coming," there's no joke coming. You are Satan's spawn filling the world with bile and garbage. Kill yourself. It's the only way to save your soul, kill yourself… I know what all the marketing people are thinking right now too, "Oh, you know what Bill's doing, he's going for that anti-marketing dollar. That's a good market, he's very smart"…Goddamnit, I'm not doing that, you scum-bags! Quit putting a goddamn dollar sign on everything on this planet!"

*disclaimer. This is a joke. Please don't actually kill yourselves, perhaps just review some of your marketing practices.

As a result of all the advertising, the free for all in this space, and with Facebook ads becoming an open platform since 2009, it has many of us now spiralling into a **social media vortex of doom**.

I think Facebook are waking up to this at the moment. I hope that in light of the recent data scandal they are wanting to make a change. I think it marks an interesting turning point for the social network, and I am interested to see how things develop from here. In case you don't know what I am talking about, the low-down is that Facebook have been collecting our data in numerous ways for years. They are tracking our activity, and building profiles on us based on this data, and it isn't just how we are behaving on Facebook itself that they are collecting. They are accumulating data and information all over the web about our habits and preferences via all of the pages and apps where Facebook has been integrated using widgets or plugins that help us to login via or share, like and comment on Facebook remotely. They are then using this to reach you with targeted adverts and 'sponsored posts' that you are seeing lots of in your Facebook and Instagram timelines.

Also enter Cambridge Analytica and other companies like them, who 'harvested' said data", to help create so-called psychographic modelling techniques."

"The belief in Silicon Valley and certainly our belief at that point was that the general public must be aware that their data is being sold and

shared and used to advertise to them," Mr. Kogan said in an interview with "60 Minutes" on Sunday." @NYTimes

Were Facebook naive? Or are we? Perhaps I am naive, but I will live in hope. Whatever the case, it is a significant point in time for us all to be more conscious of what is going on behind the scenes and to be more aware moving forward.

Timelines

Here is a quick overview of the timeline of the Age of Social Media, to give it some perspective, as I have witnessed it on a widespread scale:

MySpace launched in 2003.
Facebook in 2004.
YouTube - 2006.
Twitter - 2006.
Tumblr - 2007 (I LOVED Tumblr back in the day! It's where GIFs really started)
Instagram - 2010
Facebook bought Instagram in 2012, just 18 months later, for 1billion$.
Pinterest - 2010
Snapchat - 2011.
Instagram Stories (within the app but still good to know) - 2016

N.B There were popular localised social networks such as Echo, NYC's online community which had 46,000 members and was created by Claire

Evans in 1988. If you want, like me, to geek out about that, she has a new book "Broad Band, The Untold Story of the Women Who Made The Internet."

By writing this I want to chart some of the phases and the background to where we have come from and where we are now with social media… In a very short space of time.

I think both it, and we, are ready to evolve to a new phase in our evolution. That in our becoming conscious to the old paradigm patriarchal ways that social media is being polluted, and by us making a choice not to use social media ourselves in that same way, we can create a change.

We are back to being the change that we want to see in the world. When each of us makes a change on the individual level we collectively create bigger changes *en masse*. Now it might be that the old paradigm will continue to exist and that our own new world and way of being, will be created as a kind of parallel universe. We exist in filter bubbles (both online and offline really), but in the age of social media this is taken to another level.

*"A **filter bubble** is a state of intellectual isolation that can result from personalized searches when*

a website algorithm selectively guesses what information a user would like to see based on information about the user, such as location, past click-behavior and search history. As a result, users become separated from information that disagrees with their viewpoints, effectively isolating them in their own cultural or ideological bubbles."
- Wikipedia

The Filter bubble effect receives criticism, suggesting that it may have negative implications for society and that it played its part in Donald Trump's election as President of the USA and the Brexit vote in the UK. On a personal level it can be disruptive as well because we can think that the opinions we see in our social media microcosm are the only ones that exist when they are not.

As with all things, there are often two sides to the coin. Like I have already shared in previous chapters, filtering what we see in our timelines can be a healthy practice. Honouring our energy and our space, working with the algorithms to tell them what we like and what we don't like so that we have a better experience when we are on social media. By filling up our feeds with people and information that lights us up, not drags us down.

I have recently moved to the town of Glastonbury, England, renowned for being a spiritual home to hippies and magical folk. They sell essential oils instead of sweets at shop counters and you can't walk more than five meters without encountering the sweet scent of incense wafting through the air. You could consider that I have chosen to live in a filter bubble. Being in this environment lights me up, whereas living in the big City of London was dragging me down. I made a choice. When we make the choice to choose certain environments to be in, it doesn't need to make us less aware of what else is happening in the world. I choose to live in and be around certain environments and energies that are good for my well-being in many dimensions.

Moving forward from the Age of Social Media to Social Media for a New Age, is about making a choice. Choosing to show up differently, choosing to do what **feels** good, choosing to do what **is** good, and filtering out or changing what isn't.

It's our choice. We are the wave of change.

INNER UNICORN QUESTION TIME.

How can I honour what I know and where I am in my own journey?

How can I be part of the evolution of social media ?

How can I be the change I want to see in the world through my social media?

Chapter Six

SOCIAL MEDIA FOR A NEW AGE

If light is information
and we are in the age of information,
then we are also in the age of light.
If love is light,
then love is information,
which means we are in the age of love.
If social media is a place
for us to share information,
it is a place for us to share our light
and our love.
When we share our information
(light and love)
creatively and consciously,
we connect with
and create our commUNITY.

The world is changing, we are moving into a new age, a new earth, and social media is playing a big part in it.

We are currently in the midst of a relatively new "Information Age".

*"The **Information Age** (also known as the Computer **Age**, Digital **Age**, or New Media **Age**) is a period in human history characterised by the shift from traditional industry that the Industrial Revolution brought through industrialisation, to an economy based on **information** computerisation."*
- Wikipedia.

But there is another New Age as prophesied by many of our world religions and by the position of our planet in the cosmos, the Age of Aquarius. The Age of Aquarius is about new values of **love, community and integrity.**

*"**Age of Aquarius**" is an astrological term denoting either the current or forthcoming astrological age, depending on the method of calculation. Astrologers maintain that an astrological age is a product of the earth's slow precessional rotation and lasts for 2,160 years, on average (26,000-year period of precession / 12 zodiac signs = 2,160 years)."*
- Wikipedia

The beginning of the new Aquarian Age was November 11, 2011 or 11/11/11, and some people also believe it to be December 21, 2012. In astrology an Age lasts for 2,160 years, so we are only just tip-toeing our baby toe into it.

If we acknowledge both the Age of Information and the Age of Aquarius, then Social Media is right in the middle of this particular New Age sandwich.

As author, Lisa Lister said to me recently; *"social media is the lens that we currently look at the world through."* Mainstream media used to be the lens we would see the world through, which is owned and controlled in the main by big corporations and governments. Now, that's not to say that the big social media platforms and web giants are now not owned by corporations, nor that they are not in bed with governments. Because let's face it - we know that they are. And we are seeing more and more evidence of this right now as I am writing this - with the big Facebook data scandal.

One of the biggest differences that I have witnessed from working in the traditional broadcast and entertainment industry to working in social media, is ACCESSIBILITY.

Back in the day when I set up Kdot, my social media agency, we used to win clients and projects on the fact that that social media was *'access to audience'* and we could help companies and brands reach more people directly without needing traditional advertising or media channels. In *Social Media for a New Age*, I would like to reframe audience, into access to each other, access to **community.**

Diana Cooper is prolific in writing about the New Age. In one of her books '*Birthing a New Civilisation, Transition to the Golden Age,*' she writes about how...

"*Between now and 2032 we are undergoing a planetary house move to a much bigger home which needs deep foundations.* **We are currently clearing out the old and deciding what we want to take with us and what we want to leave behind.** *The planet itself needs cleansing and the financial, industrial, business, school and housing systems need to be reviewed and updated. We do not have very long to affect this change. We are moving into a new world of* **community spirit,** *ecological awareness, abundance-consciousness, working for the* **highest good,** *helping nature, children and creativity.*" *@dianacooperangels*

And I believe we can use social media and technology to support us in creating **community spirit** and to bring about **abundance-consciousness** on this planet of ours.

We can be the change we want to see in the world by expressing and sharing our true essence, by being an example, for the new world, for the highest good of all. Creatively and peacefully clearing and cancelling out the power hold the old patriarchal paradigm has had upon this planet.

I work with many people who are diligently helping us, and the earth, move into this new age. Each of them are doing this with their different modalities of work in the world, but all of it is working towards this.

Writing this book is my contribution towards this shift of ages, especially with social media playing such a large part of our day to day. It is important for us to approach our social media consciously, as we would other parts of our lives.

When we create content for social media, we are sharing information, whether that is in the form of the written word, video, podcasts or visual information through graphics and memes. We are sharing our essence, our creativity, our light and our love.

This is Social Media for a New Age.

Our words, when they are written down, are powerful.

Our tones when we speak and we sing, are powerful.

Our stories when we share them, are powerful.

And our actions, when we lead by example, are powerful.

I will talk more about how we are connected by this web we weave on social media. It is energetic as well as digital and I really feel that when it is used with good intentions, we are creating and sending ripples through this inter(connected) net - this world wide web. Feel the power and the vibration behind each of the words we have given to describe the digital landscape...

World Wide Web.
Inter-net.
Cyber-space.

Dani Katz is an illustrator and writer, she designed the Social Media Angel and Unicorn you see in this book and she has recently published a book on the power of our language called *"The New P* Handbook - Little Languaging Hacks for Big Change"* (P* =paradigm). I love this excerpt she shared on social media...

"Despite all reductive, left brained patriarchal paradigms to the contrary, we humans aren't just meat-suit encased monkey minds driven by intellect and that good ol' biological imperative. Rather, we are multi-dimensional beings - as abstract, intuitive and emotional as we are linear, rational and logical sending and receiving various levels and layers of information that speak to all of our complex aspects with our every word."

- @danikatz - Taken from The New P. Handbook Vol.1 : Little Languaging Hacks For Big Change

So much of what we are taught about digital media, digital marketing and social media is the "*linear, rational + logical*" elements, and not the "*abstract, intuitive, emotional*" part, where we are "*sending and receiving various levels and layers of information that speaks to all of our complex aspects with every word.*"

Social Media for a New Age is about becoming much more aware of ourselves as the multi-dimensional beings that we are and how we are receiving and how we are transmitting information and energy digitally through social media.

If you hang out in some of the circles that I do you may hear the following being referred to in conjunction with or as a response to what others are posting or is being posted online.

Being "triggered" – is usually when negative emotions are brought up such as jealously, irritation... other... This was a very popular term in relation to social media content over the past few years.

"I had to stop following X because they were just triggering me too much."

Being "activated" - is usually a positive reaction which includes the receiving of information psychically or energetically.

"I just listened to/watched X's podcast/ Facebook Live - and was totally activated by their meditation/sharing/conversation."

Sharing a "download" - posting information received from spirit or source energy. Not to be confused with digital content actually downloaded from the inter web itself but rather information received from the non-digital collective consciousness...

"I got a download earlier. [insert name of angel, spirit guide, higher self, galactic being or other]

gave me this information and I just had to share it with you all."

Sharing a "transmission" - something that is visually (art, images, symbols, photographs) or audibly, verbally (words, sounds, tones, light language) encoded with information that effects the recipient in a positive way.

"Can you see the violet rays of light in that photograph? They just transmitted some powerful healing to you."

You might also hear about 'upgrades', not to be confused with the digital kind. In the same way your operating system provider asks you to 'download upgrades' to improve your phone or laptop - people online are also offering and sharing content and conversations as a way to help us 'upgrade' our consciousness.

I find it so interesting that we are using language derived for the digital era when communicating about our more multidimensional and spiritual activities online (and offline) and that this language has become somewhat blurred between the spiritual and digital.

If you have any others that spring to mind, please message me on Instagram @katiekdot_socialmediaangel

THE INTERNET IS
A HIVE MIND

As is the data collected every moment by our devices by the likes of Facebook and Google…

"hive mind":

1. a notional entity consisting of a large number of people who share their knowledge or opinions with one another, regarded as producing either uncritical conformity or collective intelligence.

- Google Dictionary

Remembering this is useful when navigating our own journey on social media…

How we access it,
How we affect it,
How we let it affect us,
How we use it for the greater good of all.

"The internet was gifted to Earth to help with the problem of critical mass. When taken collectively this web, internet, connect to the interior of the unification force we call Oneness and permeate with light the Form's Formless consciousness."
- Ashtar through Elizabeth Trutwin, January 17, 2017

I'm just going to leave that one there, to let it do its thing - to transmit, upgrade and activate ya! ;)

INNER UNICORN QUESTION TIME

What does Social media for a new age mean to me and my social media strategy?

If I think of the internet as another dimension how does that shift my relationship to it?

How can I use my social media platform to support the evolution of the planet and its people?

Chapter 7

A STRATEGY OF LOVE

I place love at the centre of my
social media strategy,
creating community,
honouring integrity.
I am part of a new age,
helping the planet onto the next stage.

I have been using a strategy of love for a while now with my clients and on my own social media and it gets great results and feedback...

"Possibly the best lesson on social media strategy out there."
- Paul Hornsey-Pennel via Facebook Groups Growth & Engagement.

The magic happens when you...

Love yourself.
Love your offering.
Love creating.
Love your community.
Love connecting.
Love curating.
Love sharing.
Love showing up.
Love rising.
Love serving.
Love supporting.
Love giving.
Love receiving.
Love being.
Love journeying.

Remembering that fear is an energy that contracts (e.g. the social media vortex of doom) and love is an energy that expands, it is logical that having a strategy of love for your social media is going to help you to expand your message, your community and much more.

"As you continue to send out love, the energy returns to you in a regenerating spiral... As love accumulates, it keeps your system in balance and harmony. Love is the tool, and more love is the end product." Sara Paddison (author of *The Hidden Power of the Heart: Discovering an Unlimited Source of Intelligence*)

Love is one of the most powerful energies on our planet and it is absolutely free to give and to receive.

'The Power of Love' was the title of the powerful and rousing sermon at the wedding of Prince Harry and Meghan Markle, which wasn't just in reference to romantic love but the power that love has to change the world.

"The late Dr. Martin Luther King once said, and I quote, "We must discover the power of love, the redemptive power of love, and when we do that, we will make of this old world a new world". Love is the only way. There's power in love. Don't underestimate it. Don't even over sentimentalise it. There's power, power in love... If you don't believe me, just stop and think and imagine, think and imagine, well, think and imagine a world where love is the way. Imagine our homes and families when love is the way. Imagine neighbourhoods and

communities where love is the way. Imagine governments and nations where love is the way. Imagine business and commerce when love is the way. Imagine this tired old world when love is the way."
- Most Reverend Michael Bruce Curry

If you are aware of how energy flows, remembering this power of love for your social media can make a huge difference to your offering. We often forget, or don't make the connection that what is true for our physical, and spiritual world is also true for our digital world. This is particularly useful when we go into fear or frustration with social media, and things do not flow.

For the more sensitive amongst us we can FEEL when content is coming from that place of fear or from the heart. Speaking to this, I'm very blessed that author Lisa Lister is not only my friend, but my editor and chief cheerleader for this book, she sends me little updates on what's working for her on social media… This text popped in a few weeks back;

"Reporting in, when I only post things on social media that feel fun + fill me up + are in alignment with my message (women, we're cyclic + powerful and a reflection of mumma nature + the cosmos)

I post WITH love + nourishment + it's received that way too. Hurrah! "

But there have been times when I am working with clients and there is a need, or an expectation for a launch to go well, or make a certain amount of money, which sends them into a fear dynamic. This fear energy then gets transmuted into the content they create, and you can sense this in the posts.

These expectations have been created by the digital marketing expert industry itself, that making six figures on a launch is the norm, and that by 'doing what they did' you can do it too. We have been absorbing this kind of messaging, particularly over the past few years through adverts and lead magnets selling their expertise on how to do this. These experts have studied this stuff on a strategic and psychological level which watches and learns what the 'hive mind' responds to. They are often not really viewing us as real people, on the other side of the screen. There is nothing new about that, big business has been viewing us as numbers on a spreadsheet for eons. And on some level (if you want to get mind-melty here), nature can be viewed as numbers too. I went out with a quantum physicist who could read the whole universe through numbers. Again, who is right and what is wrong here? Neither. But not all of us are quantum physicists or accountants who can see or work with the world in this way.

Is it possible to have big numbers and still remember that it is real people on the other side of your screen, on the other side of your marketing? Of course it is. I see clients managing the dance of this very well when they use a strategy of love.

It can be as simple as having that reminder, the conscious awareness, that it is a real human being, a spirit, a soul who is receiving your information, your transmission, your content, your advert, your email, your blog, your posts.

As simple as remembering that YOU now, in this new age, feel, sense and know when something is just a strategy, or marketing, or a sales pitch.

ADAPT AND PIVOT FROM THIS POINT

There is nothing at all wrong at all with marketing or selling but in this now age, particularly on social media which is a social **NETWORK**, how we connect and engage with each other here is paramount. Numbers without the relationship isn't working in quite the same way anymore. Community, connection and relationships, which can be created online or otherwise, with a strategy of love, is where things are moving to.

Just last week I had a catch up coaching call with a client, who came on with a heavy heart sharing with me how she had just delivered a 'BIG Launch' of a three-month program that had totally bombed out. I asked her why she thought it has happened that way… And she said…

"I was busy doing what I thought I was supposed to do, rather than do what I felt I should do. I was busy doing what I had seen other people doing, I forgot to connect, and I went into sell, sell, sell".

When we infuse our social media content and strategy with the energy of love, and focus on that, it is only a matter of time (divine time, not always your timing) before that energy is returned. I have seen some really interesting cases of this in action. Someone thinking they are ready for social media stardom and success, trying to make it happen, but the truth of it being that they still had some work to do before being ready for things to take off. Perhaps there were things they still needed to learn, systems they still needed to put in place before things were ready to take that leap forward. And I have seen how when someone is really ready, when they are in the zone, and don't need it to happen 'their way', it is more often than not pretty effortless. We need to show up, and there needs to be substance of course, but when it's your time, it drops into place just as it is meant to.

Divine timing; it can be a total bitch when we really want something to happen, on our perceived timeline, but surrendering and letting go more often than not helps things to manifest. Be it boyfriends or book deals!

So, when you surrender and show up with your strategy of love, it is good to remember that the energy you put in may not be returned to you in thousands of followers or likes, or even dollars (although often it does). These are the reward mechanisms we have been programmed to want by an industry who in turn want to sell us the 'how to' courses and products.

Instead it might just come back to you in much subtler but much more magical and meaningful ways.

I have lots of stories about ways my clients (and myself) have received both financially and otherwise from the love and care put into social media, but it is not always straightforward.

Maureen @maureen_sharphouse and I were working together to create a new content plan to build her audience. Maureen is a real natural on video and we came up with a video content plan that mirrors her coaching work. She works a lot with mantras so we decided on 'Morning Mantras' as a video series. As with all things it takes time for new content to build in engagement and at first the engagement and the reach was pretty low to start off with. On a catch up call we were discussing the returns re time and energy etc. Maureen said it didn't matter about the engagement, she *"trusted and loved"* what she was doing. A couple of days later I get an email from her saying she had received a message from someone who said they had been watching, this person had not been commenting or even liking the posts, but she wanted to sign up to one of Maureen's top coaching packages. Definitely a return on investment! But it doesn't always have to be a financial return.

Remember me telling you about how I met my dear friend Gail Love Schock thanks to Instagram? Her friendship is priceless to me. I don't think we can put a price on the community and connection that has come for many of us from social media. It's a really good thing to remember and be grateful for.

If you have a strategy of love and are sharing your light (and your shadow) authentically, then you will attract people, collaborations, friends, clients that are in alignment with you, your work and where you are at on your unique journey.

"Just as a lily pad in a pond will rise and fall on the wave produced by a pebble dropped in that pond, so acts of kindness will raise the spirits of people we might never know."
- David R. Hamilton PhD – Author of *Why Kindness is Good for You*

Someone that I would consider having a strategy of love is the astrologer I mentioned previously, Kaypacha. I haven't worked with him personally, but I love watching his videos every week.

No complicated strategy.
No need to use lots of hashtags.
No email list building or big sales strategy.
No clever copy.
No formulas.
Good content.
Connected content.
Knows himself and his community.

The content he creates connects him with the collective regularly, which serves them and serves him, by increasing his visibility, allowing him to let people know what things he has going on, should they want to connect with him in different ways.

I get people sharing his videos with me on WhatsApp, messenger and everywhere in-between - because he knows his stuff and he is helping to educate, inform and support people though his work.

He is creating content that is *"also good for people's well-being and for society."*

As a result of that, he doesn't need to 'sell' his workshops or his membership website. People want to go to his events or purchase his content because they have got to know him, like him and trust him from his videos. For me this is great example of this new age of social media, and who better to be leading the way than someone like Kaypacha?

It is not just the information he shares but **his energy, his vibe**…

"Namaste. Aloha. So much love."

We can make social media really complicated for ourselves if we want to. And many of us do. I am not immune to over-complicating sometimes. It is usually when I **over-think** it, or look at what everyone else is doing… Or if I am **trying** to please a client or **trying** to build numbers or **trying** to sell something.

Over thinking it can mean that we 'think' we have to post every day, or three times a day, and that we have to be in people's timelines ALL the time for them to see us, to see the value in us, to remember us, to want to buy from or work with us. Actually, all it might take is one blog post, one video, one sharing and you are there, already in their hearts, connection made. (In fact, over-posting could have the opposite effect on this connection!)

Or we might think we have to be 'teaching' or giving tons of value all the time when sharing our truth may just be enough. (Over-givers and 'helpers' might recognise this one - I know it's something I've had to lean into.)

Complicating it might look like you think you need all of the fancy tools before you can get started, the right camera, lighting, make up, outfit, location, film crew, professional photos, branding etc. When actually you just need to whip out your mobile phone and stand by a window in order to capture some really authentic video content, with good lighting. We often think that it has to be perfect, and polished in order for it to be successful when actually how you make people feel is what really matters.

"I've learned that people will forget what you said, people will forget what you did, but people will never forget how you made them feel."
- Maya Angelou

All of my biggest and best successes have been when I have NOT been trying to do anything, other than show up with **passion** and **love.**

When we won the Sony Radio Award, that podcast was something we **LOVED** doing. We weren't trying to win an award, we wanted to keep reaching the community that the guys had in radio and clubland, about music we loved, whilst keeping them on the radio as that was something they loved too.

It all came from a place of total **LOVE.**

I always try to look at what is in front of me, responding to what is happening and what people are feeling or loving.

What can we do that is easy?
What can we do that is in alignment?
What do people **love**?
Let's do more of that.

LOVE IN ACTION

*"When you make service an expression of **love,** the Universe shall exalt you."*
- Universal Kabbalah.

Jordan Gray is a blogger I have been following for the past few years. Apart from having a little crush on him for being awesome, I have also enjoyed watching him play with social media. This guy gets over a million hits to his blog and is currently smashing it up on YouTube as well. He got an email from someone recently that he shared on his Instagram Stories where someone had told him his blog *"has changed my life forever"*.

Jordan comments, *"Seriously feeling blessed. Humble brag or not... I get to live out my mission everyday of supporting people in their love lives. I sincerely hope you get to experience this kind of alignment in your life and that you have a deep sense of meaning in your actions".*
- @jordan_gray_consulting

And when we add together, the age of social media, with social media for a new age, your social media soul and a strategy of love we get…

Fifth Density (5D) Existence

Ego-less; Service to others; Actions based on love; Unconditional love; Ongoing gratitude; Self-realized; Fearless; No limits; Unity-minded; Recognise self as part of the whole; Manifestation easy; Goes with the flow; Duality & linear time dissolves; Only time is now; No need for possessions or status." Taken from Indigo Awakening Facebook group

There are many, **infinite, limitless** ways to be successful in life and on social media. If we all adopted a strategy of love can you imagine what we could achieve collectively?

INNER UNICORN QUESTION TIME

How is my social media content good for people's well-being and society?

How can I create meaningful connections between people online rather than adding to the passive consumption of content?

What do people love about me and/or my offerings?

Chapter 8

VISIBILITY VULNERABILITIES

Am I bragging or showing off?
Am I boring?
Am I good enough?
When you show up and share
from your heart,
You are sharing your soul,
your gifts and your art.
When you set your intentions
and get clear on your why,
Your content will reach
the right timelines,
The right hearts,
the right eyes.

Sharing our information, our light, our love, our lives, our passion, our medicine... Especially in the name of 'marketing' ourselves, is a much more scary and complex thing than we often give it credit for. And as part of our strategy of love, it calls on us to really love ourselves. Hard.

Learning how to show up in public, in groups and communities is something we are all being schooled on in some form or other through the nature of social media. From a personal development perspective, working on your fears of being visible and being seen is an aspect of it that can be very rewarding to explore and move through.

Being visible, authentic, sharing yourself on social media can generate and activate many layers and fears, that can and will stop a lot of people from really sharing their gifts. But when you are able to share your gifts through your creativity and your creations, sharing them with a pure resonance, without fear or lack, your essence and energy will then attract to it your highest good.

You know you have something to share with the world...

Be it art, music, poetry, healing... But we are scared. Scared of what people will think, scared of the unknown. Scared of failure.

Someone left this comment for me on an Instagram about this;

"I've literally started a new public account tonight with a view to sharing in this way, but I've been debating it all week. I'm embarrassed for friends to see, I'm scared to be vulnerable, or to share too much with too many people etc. But something bigger than all of the above is making me want to do it despite my fears. Still definitely very real fears though."

Loving yourself, seeing yourself, learning about yourself, becoming conscious to yourself is another awesome side effect of this being on social media. Your confidence is likely to increase the more you engage with the process, and comfier you get with it. This confidence then has the opportunity to spill across and have a positive effect across many elements of your life, including the added bonus of learning the art of **not caring what other people think of you.**

"The more we become ourselves, speak and share it outwardly - the more we have to learn to love that fear within. That fear of being too much, of being too different, of being too seen or too free."

- Sophie Gregroire @sophieg_ journeyauthenticself

I have experienced this for myself. It was only a few years ago that I decided to start to share online, as me, and build a personal "profile" and brand.

Video was one of my biggest fears, which is very common. I remember thinking, I'll start doing videos when I have lost some weight or *insert another excuse* for not doing it. It also made me REALLY nervous. Like really, really nervous – throat would close, brain would shut down nervous.

This shows up a lot when I'm working 1-2-1 with clients, I mention video, and in particular Live video, as part of the content mix and I see their whole body language change and shut down.

Often it feels like it is a fear of feeling exposed, of being judged, of being seen, of not being engaging enough, good enough, of people not watching, of nerves getting the better of them in moment… etc. Which is why I always suggest playing, practicing and getting comfortable with video before posting or going live.

A lot of people are surprised when I tell them about my fears of being seen, because I seem so confident in my videos. I do really love doing videos now, I enjoy it very much, but to begin with I felt totally exposed.

I have often thought of video work as a kind of mirror work therapy, that one of my clients Mexican shaman Sergio Magaña teaches in his book the The Toltec Secret, as do Louise Hay and Robert Holden.

Video holds a lot of magic for your platforms, because if you can break through these fears and start to connect with people through video content and feel really comfortable with it, you can build relationships with people quickly and effectively, whether it be pre-recorded or on live.

How I got through my fears looked a little like this…

I got some help.

In my one of my 'Conversations on Social Media For A New Age' Podcasts I chat to one of my oldest friends, sports coach and teacher Jamie Barnwell about this and other learning and coaching techniques that you can adapt for your social media strategy. He is the one who helped me move through my fears. You can find it on soundcloud.com/socialmediaangel. Essentially it was about practice, and practicing under different sets of conditions, such as really fast or really slow, that helped me to break through my blocks.

Once I had broken through some of my initial resistance using Jamie's coaching techniques, I was able to then play and practice on my own. I found ways to make it fun and enjoyable, which meant getting out into nature, the beach, fun locations and finding environments that made me feel safe.

That feeling of safety was key for me. I noticed that I looooved FaceTime and Zoom calls and that actually recording videos for my social media was just like that and that I had nothing to fear. I thought about people I knew when I was recording and imagined them on the other side of the screen, which helped me be more natural with my delivery.

I usually recommend to clients that they play and practise first before publishing. Finding your own happy place so that your content is infused with confidence and your joy. I would recommend getting out into nature, taking your camera / phone and a selfie stick. Making it playful for me means going to hang out with the faeries in the woods or meadows, or with the mermaids on the beach and asking them to help me find my flow with creating video. I also do things like taking a few of my favourite crystals with me, some wisdom cards to guide me and essential oils for my pulse points. Root

& Flower @root_and_flower do some beautiful ones for the chakra points, one I like to work with is the Crown chakra, which comes with a little affirmation, *"I am aware, connected and wise"*. Then, I ask my guides and my higher self what information wants to come through and I write some notes, ideas and topics, whip my camera out and start filming. Once I've got some good stuff on film, I can decide which ones I want to post.

I can get a bit overexcited and want to post everything all at once, but it is good to then take some time and watch through (this helps you get comfy with seeing yourself on camera - I actually make myself smile rather than wince to watch back now!) and then make a plan for when to post the ones that feel best to you and that you are proud to share.

Remember that we do not have to share everything in the name of authenticity. We don't want just to show all the perfect things, we want to be real, but we also want to tune into when we post and how much we post.

Professionalism is good to remember depending on your line of work, something that I think we have begun to forget about when it comes to being online, because so many walls and barriers are being dissolved through the very nature of social media and the popularity of celebrity style reality TV shows, and as we explore what it means to be authentic and vulnerable. It is good, in fact often better, to not over produce your content in this instant, authentic, digital age. However, let's still be discerning and thoughtful about what we share.

It is personal choice, but sharing your personal life online rather than sharing your gifts, skills and wisdom are two very different things. Some people do both very well, but it still becomes a little weird and has some blurry lines. I have had sessions with people who are paralysed by the thought of having to share about their lives in order to be on social media. I have others where they feel they are showing up too much and feel they want to reign it in.

It is a balance and each of us will feel differently about this. Each of us have different businesses, different things we want to share with our audiences.

Tamara aka @_wolfsister had a valuable exchange with me about this on email recently when I was posting about authenticity and marketing. I am going to be talking about this in more detail in a few chapters' time too, so hang fire to get into that juicy topic! But in relation to the blurred lines between business, marketing and sharing ourselves on social media authentically, Tamara, who is a crystal healer and author of The Crystal Code, had this to say;

"I think that with the uprise in solopreneurs, then we are our own brand/product and so the lines get blurred. People are sharing what's happening in their personal lives, and in effect their whole 'grid' becomes marketing. I'm still figuring out how I navigate this with my own work. Ultimately, what I'm 'selling' is intertwined with the way that I live my life."

For Tamara, as a healer and intuitive, sharing her practices and her tools is intertwined between her personal life, her business life and her social media marketing. But she can still have boundaries about how much she shares of her personal and private life online.

It really is a personal choice. Listen to your body and tune into your mind chatter whenever you post on social media. It will tell you what is the right balance of personal content, of your life, and how/if it relates to the reason you are on social media, to your business, to your gifts, to your mission or your message.

If when you post it makes you feel really uncomfortably vulnerable and exposed, then explore that.

If when you post, you feel like you aren't really sharing your essence or your voice, that your post just feels a bit 'meh' or formulaic or doesn't light you up… Explore that.

Look at your frequency of posts and tune into if it feels good **to you**. You might be a prolific poster who shares everything they see and feel on Insta stories and actually that feels great, you get a lot from it, your audience gets a lot from it and so everyone's a winner, baby.

But you might tune in and think *"oh no I just threw up all over Instagram and even I'm doing my own head in, what's this all about then?"*

You also might take a look and realise that it is a barren wasteland of nothingness and you need to step your visibility up in order to actually connect with people. When you are connecting with people and building a relationship through your content, then being true to you and being who you are, will as in *your vibe attracts your tribe*, attract the right people for you, to you.

We of course need to be present online for people to find us and get to know us, our products and services, and the nature of platforms such as Instagram stories and Snapchat are all about the sharing of our day to day… These blurred lines can touch our visibility vulnerability nerves in so many different and unique ways.

There are lots of complications to being visible online.

You may not want everyone knowing what you are up to, and where you are all of the time - plain and simple! And why should you have to share that? You don't. We create our own boundaries.

Setting boundaries is an art, but once you have felt into what feels good for you to share, and how often, becoming conscious of if you are stepping outside of, or into, those is the next step.

I bought a very nice green juice the other day and for a half a second I thought about sharing it on Instagram stories. I know when I share 'lifestyle' choices, that I feel more often than not like a bit of a dick afterwards, so I have learnt to stop myself before I actually post something, then regret it later.

Another boundary I have put in place is how often I share on social media when I am hanging out with friends. When friends also happen to be well known or recognisable to your community, this can get a bit sticky and feel a bit weird, so it is one to look out for. My friendship with Lisa Lister for example, all of our hang time is not for sharing on social media, some of it is sacred. It's nice to share some of the together times with your peeps, but some of it can sometimes feel a bit 'ooh look at me with all my cool / well known friends' which can feel a bit 'name drop-y'. So, keep an eye on it, see how it feels. On occasions of course, it is fun to take a selfie (x 500) and share it with the world, but ask; 'what's the intention?'

Is this coming from my social media soul or social media ego?

You get to choose how much you share, what you share, who you share it with and when you share it. Sharing your life does not necessarily mean finding your voice about your topic or expertise, although you can use sharing about relevant things in your life to help you find your authentic voice. You just don't have to tell everyone what you had for breakfast or how many workouts you have done today. *

*Unless you are a nutritionist or a fitness coach perhaps.

If you identify with being more of an introvert than an extrovert, the thought of oversharing can be a terrifying aspect to social media. It can be really tough to show up and be present in a space which feels like everyone else has their shit together, and you don't feel like that, or you feel like you really do not even want to be seen. It can be tough to find and share your voice.

Visibility vulnerability can stop people from getting started and it can stop people from being consistent. Sometimes the feeling lasts, sometimes it is cyclical. We need to talk about it, so we can learn about it and so we can lean into it, work with it and shift it, if that is right for us.

If you have a womb it could be linked with your monthly cycle. (Please look to Lisa and her book *Code Red* for all the information on this.) For me, when I'm bleeding, I have nothing to share with the world on social media, however when I am ovulating I have everything to share with the world on social media.

I've noticed how the weather and the seasons effect my activity too. This year as I came back to England in winter, my desire to show up and share pretty much disappeared. I went into a space and place of hibernation. This is very natural though - bears hibernate during winter after all, I'll take that bear medicine and run with it.

Oh, and full moons, new moons, portals, solar flares, eclipses, energy waves, retrogrades – yup, count them in too!

It is all natural. A lot of us go into hibernation. It doesn't break the internet, nor does it break our platforms, reach or engagement. In fact, in some cases it creates the opposite effect - a significant increase in engagement and reach when coming back online, rested and revived, missed by followers, friends and fans.

NOTHING BAD HAPPENS IF YOU DON'T POST

Just because authenticity and vulnerability are buzz words all over social media doesn't mean we have to share everything with everyone, just as we don't share everything with everyone in our lives.

Some things are simply sacred.

We can honour the shit out of that sacredness.

I pulled right back from Instagram stories for a while for this very reason. I had to ask my inner unicorn these questions...

Why am I sharing this?
What am I showing up for?
What am I using social media as a tool for?
What I am being visible on social
media about?
What I am getting vulnerable about?
What is authentic here?

When I get really real with myself; I am on social media to share about being a social media coach and about *Social Media For A New Age*, to connect with people and share about that topic. I am not here to be a social media celebrity. I am on social media to connect with my clients, to connect with my community, to reach out and share my learnings, my ideas, my insight and my artistry and to attract people to the medicine, and the work I am doing in the world. It was then I realised I needed to get back on mission. I am not online to share about my personal life or my lifestyle preferences. Sharing about our lifestyle choices, unless it is relevant and no matter how tempting, can be a real distraction from our mission.

It's tough this one though. I was just leaning out my study window watching the world go past on a Saturday morning on Glastonbury High Street, when a Shetland pony and a woman with a little lamb were suddenly outside my window… My hand reached instantly for my phone and before I know it, I've shared it on Stories.

This has in part come from the habit of see it, snap it, share it. And I know that my friends, community and connections will enjoy receiving some energy from the heart chakra of the planet and what makes me smile will make them smile.

So, what is my intention behind that post? To make others smile the same way I am smiling? OK cool. I'll allow that. But the yoga poses, the breakfast bowls, the tropical beach locations, the set-up photos made just for social media... I have to question *why* we do it. I've been there, right alongside everyone posting pics of my laptop in lovely locations, sipping on coconuts by the pool, feeling all fancy... But a lot of it is a projection. An ideal. It is a simply a snapshot, which can take us off track, a distraction that takes us away from showing up for the things we are really meant to be sharing.

An uneasy feeling hit me pretty hard when I started sharing my travel experiences on my Instagram stories... People had asked me to share photos of my travels which had made me want to do it and it is fun to share adventures, grid points, sights and sounds with the people who love you, with my friends in my pocket...

Plus 'strategically' with the marketing head on, it does look good and it lets you know a bit more about me on a personal level… HOWEVER, I came to an abrupt halt with sharing in this way for a good few months while I thought about my WHY.

Before you go to make a post on social media, ask your inner unicorn the same questions…

Why is this relevant?
What am I doing?
What is my intention for these posts?
Am I doing this because everyone else
is doing it?
Am I doing it because it looks good?
Is this coming from my social media ego or is it
coming from my social media soul?

I am not trying to sell the laptop lifestyle and I am not a travel blogger. I made a personal choice to spend time in south east Asia for a number of reasons. Although it might have looked glamorous and on trend, it actually came about because of some not so fun personal heartbreak stuff, which I didn't share about online. Plus travelling alone was also pretty challenging and lonely at times! But I didn't share about that stuff either… So why was I OK with sharing about the other side, the positive side, of it so openly?

I really had to dig deep and listen to myself so I could find a comfortable way of moving forward with Instagram stories. I am here to help people with being online, to build a meaningful social media platform that serves them, serves their audience and serves the world with their magic and love.

Yet I am also on here to have fun, to inspire, to enjoy using the platforms for playing, creating and connecting. I want to listen to both of those voices inside of me.

WHAT AM I HERE
TO SHARE?

It is great for me to go through everything myself, it helps me explore, experience and reflect back to you my learnings, this includes trying things out and making mistakes.

Visibility vulnerability hits me all the time - it is hitting me as I am writing this book! I know that it happens for a lot of people, at different times and in different ways. I have had clients report that when they go through a phase of showing up a lot they get hit with *"vulnerability hangover"*, as we have called it, and have to take a step back for a little bit to recover.

Each of us will have our own versions that pop up in all sorts of different ways, probably even daily. It is not something to feel bad about - rather something to embrace and experiment with. It is not natural, authentic or real to think we can show up online every day, every week with the same level of energy, sharing our lives and ourselves… We have to work out what is the best rhythm and best practice for our own souls.

Personal, subjective and unique.

We are sharing and giving out not just content but also our energy online and in turn we are exposing ourselves. The more we share with others the more we can connect, but this can also leave us open to having energetic hooks attached to us. This is a real thing. Spiritual coach, author of *Be The Guru* and fellow unicorn George Lizos *@GeorgeLizos*, recorded a podcast with me about psychic attacks and cyberbullying, and how to protect ourselves from bad energy from others. Have a listen to it on soundcloud.com/socialmediaangel.

George explains, *"On a higher level we are all connected, we are all energy and there is an energetic web that connects us all, so when someone thinks a negative thought about you, some of that energy reaches you."*

I have spoken with other intuitive, spiritual friends and clients, who tell me how they can actually FEEL when people are watching their videos or reading their blogs and can pick up on the positive or negative energy.

With sharing our personal and private lives online, when we are putting ourselves out there in pieces, these pieces are then open to misinterpretation, because more often than not we don't share the whole story. EG. why I went to Thailand/travelling. This can lead to other people's stuff coming up, perhaps judging you, misreading you, making assumptions about you, that is then being projected at you, even if it is unconsciously.

"Tools to combat energetic attacks can include shielding yourself everyday, clearing your field and your aura, doing a protection spell, calling in your unicorn guides, smudging etc. Which all work with our intention. These tools are not outside of us however, it's me believing that it can protect me that actually protects me. Be your own guru, connect to your own spirituality and symbolisms, to find things that feel right for you." - @GeorgeLizos

We want to share ourselves authentically online, whilst honouring our needs, protecting our digital avatars energy, and showing a strategy of love for ourselves, even if that means coming offline for a while.

If you just want to take a few days off or even a few weeks, try sharing with your community that you are taking time off for self-care and that you will be back soon.

CLOSED FOR
SPIRITUAL MAINTENANCE

There is this great meme doing the rounds which people use when they are taking a break from being online, and from what I have seen it is always met with love, respect and care from others (and if it isn't then it is their problem, not yours!) Another option is to recycle some of your precious content. Schedule your best blogs, vlogs or other to keep things rolling while you have some time off.

Getting better at creating boundaries for when we spend time online can also really help with of this. Sonia, of @itssoniaandsabrina, co-author of

You Are Amazing, daughter to Sonia Choquette and overall nugget of loveliness, recently posted about her own practices and something that can help if you are dealing with any kind of social media vulnerability overload.

"One big thing that I practice is NOT doing social media. That means no Instagram, Facebook, messenger, or email until early afternoon. Slowing down and giving myself space before filling my head with others curated experience. Take care of your head and your heart, to slow down, to connect to your spirit and the present moment. Because if we look, all the magic, is right there."

If you struggle with being seen and sharing yourself on social media, and you know that you really want to take things to the next level with your online presence, my words of reassurance are that it does get better the more you play, practice and post. Take it slow, be really gentle with yourself around it. When you do share something, celebrate yourself, create a little reward ritual to remind yourself how well you did, each time you share your beautiful, brave soul with others.

INNER UNICORN QUESTION TIME

How does posting on social media feel in my body?

When does sharing on social media feel too much?

What protection tools can I use in my social media practice?

Chapter 9

CREATIVITY, CONTENT AND CONNECTION.

Social media is a creative dream come true,
Create pictures, articles, videos
and podcasts too.
Finding your creative flow,
helps your content to connect and glow,
And as you shine your creative light,
Watch your platforms ignite,
Tap into your inner voice, ideas or vision,
Use creative social media
to share your mission.

The creative expression of your gifts, in finding and using your voice through multimedia to express the self, the soul, the spirit, is an art form on social media. Will Smith says, when speaking about his new YouTube Vlog that;

CREATING IS A WAY OF GETTING IN SYNC WITH THE UNIVERSE

Will Smith

"I cannot believe how much YouTube has awakened me. I'm finding my voice, there's so much I wanted to say."
- @WillSmith

We are constantly creating and being creative when we are making content or posting to social media. Even how we express ourselves through gifs, and stickers in our stories. In messenger chat, I LOVE to express my spirit through the art of GIF-ing, as a creative expression of self, which we are doing even when we chat just using Emojis.

Creative communication. All of it is a form of being creative.

When I was a kid creating multimedia content was my kind of play time... I would pretend I had my own radio station, it was called FAB. I would interview people that came round to the house, using an old toaster as my satellite dish and sticking homemade posters around the house to announce that I was 'on tour'.

(= Podcasting)

Writing articles for my school magazine and poetry was a huge passion when I was at school; I won the school poetry prize when I was 17, and you can see this creative side of me come through in the Social Media Angel Mantras for this book...

(= Writing and blogging.)

As soon as I was allowed to do work experience, at age 15 or 16, I applied to work at my local community TV channel where they let me loose with a camera to create a program with my friends from my acting group. The fun we had... Writing scripts, dressing up and creating together.

(= Video production and broadcasting.)

Some people are born to work with numbers, others music, art, cooking, sport etc. When it comes to our creativity, our talents and expression we all are different but we all have one thing in common, and that is the creative spark which exists within all of us.

When we choose and are able to share this creative spark on social media, it becomes a point of attraction for manifestation. There should never be a limit to our creativity, we have to give it space and time to explore at different points in our lives. Having a creative outlet is good for our health and well-being, as is connection. Social media is totally winning in that regard.

It gives us a wonderful opportunity to be creative and share it with others, which is only getting easier and easier, as tech gets better and better.

"When your heart is suggesting a new idea or creative outlet in your life, it is showing you possible joy in the realising of it. We rarely listen to the heart the first time because the ego has many echoes in the world. Only your heart will repeat and repeat until you get it. Life will bring you by accident to different events and places that will trigger the feeling of your passion. You will get the message. And because you are connected to yourself, you will recognise your new excitement. My best advice is to listen because this is a gold nugget! Your

soul will reveal itself to you there! Jump on your idea! Go for it! Forget about the possible failure, the judgment etc... Connect to your inner source of creativity, live your passion and express yourself."
- @KarenRuimy

EXPRESS YOUR
ESSENCE CREATIVELY

When expressing your essence and creativity through social media content, the tone, the vibe, the look and feel of it is something I talk a lot about in my workshops and with my clients. It is how people recognise and remember you.

Creating content is not a comfortable or easy thing for many to do. I get a lot of messages about the wasted time trying to figure out photoshop or even online programs like Canva. Then the thought of editing a video or a podcast can sometimes be a real block to getting online with new creative multimedia content. In this case it can be best to hire, collaborate and consult people / agencies / freelancers and beyond to help you with the production aspects. Where possible, build a team around you of supporters and helpers, other like-minded souls, who are tapping into their own creative gifts and passions. I don't think Will Smith spends time editing his vlogs, he will have a team to help him produce his content.

I'm not talking about making it all super shiny and glossy either, but more about not allowing anything to stop you from the having the space to explore areas of creative expression that are available to us. If using tech and making content isn't your thing, you are probably wasting time trying to figure out how to do it, especially if that thing does not bring you joy, so find someone to work with, who does.

If you do hire a team, or someone to help you with content creation, you absolutely want to be involved in the process. Do not just hand it over to someone else to decide on. You want to be at the centre point wherever possible, especially when it is a personal brand. Ideally you will create the raw content, and you will share your ideas, thoughts and dreams with your team, which can then be edited and produced into something more, supporting you by bringing your ideas into existence.

Many of us try to do it all – I definitely do sometimes – but I have a great VA, Sandi @ planetsandi, who supports me with my clients' content production for their platforms.

I, however, can be a bit of a control freak when it comes to my own content. I know I am not alone in this.

There are so many talented people who can help you create, remix, rework your magic, using your style, your flow, your glow, to help you to produce even more of the right kind of consistent content for your platforms. Make sure the people you hire are passionate about what they do *and* what you do. Make sure that they can take direction from you and are able to run with ideas on your behalf.

TEAMWORK MAKES THE DREAM WORK

I work with a graphic designer, one my best friends, Huw Mathias. Huw has a graphic design consultancy @lightworkcreate. Huw has supported me on lots of projects including designing and creating artwork, memes, banners and beyond for many of my clients, including Hay House, Diana Cooper, Karen Ruimy and Kyle Gray.

Good graphics, that share our essence and our mission through our branding, help us create an impact when publishing content. It also acts as a way of transmitting information on a multidimensional level.

Colours, symbols, images and even fonts have a resonance, a vibration, a communication which creates a connection. Creatively expressing your soul through the visuals on your social media can be subtle, and it can blatant. You can use visual threads and themes to create consistency and improve connection through your content.

It's why I commissioned Dani Katz to create an illustration of the Social Media Angel for this book. This one image is saying lots of different things on my behalf without words.

When we are scrolling our newsfeeds, we recognise and remember, these visual touch-points, and it helps to establish subtle but strong connections with our communities.

Look at the posts in your timeline and on your platforms - tune into how they feel.

What do you sense?
What happens in your body?

What is it saying?
Do you feel any sensations?
Do you feel any emotions?

These visual and sensual touch-points are powerful.

Huw has a process which he takes people through, to help them and their mission be at the very core of the design elements. He supports people develop visually creative ways to present themselves online, branding and art direction that contains their essence, helping them to connect their spirit to others.

To create successful social media and all that it is - you must create content of some kind. Content is after all the blood running through the body of social media; it is its currency, it is its nature.

PLAY IS THE GREATEST FORM OF RESEARCH

Albert Einstein.

Playing and having fun is a great way to find your creative flow, trying things out until you find YOUR thing.

"I do not believe making money in order to consume goods is mankind's sole purpose on this planet. If you're wondering what I believe our purpose on this planet is, I'll give you a hint... It has to do with creating and sharing." Bill Hicks

Social media is by its nature "to do with creating and sharing" who we are and what we do in the world.

Play, create, share, connect and have some fun.

Be that going Live on Facebook, making a podcast or writing a blog.

Copy Cats

People will copy you - it happens to every one of us at some point on social media, and to some more than others. Sometimes it's an accident ('idea hopping' - when an idea isn't realised by one person, it moves to another - is an insight from Elizabeth Gilbert's book *Big Magic*), sometimes it is unconscious, and sometimes it's on purpose. Don't let any of those things stop you from creating and sharing. If you feel someone is copying you, reach out to them with evidence and ask them to stop. If that doesn't work, report them and if that doesn't work, block them and/or seek legal advice.

No-one is YOU and it will not stop you from owning YOUR lane.

Send them love and use it as an opportunity to get even better at being yourself, trusting that no-one else can do it as well as YOU can!

"Maybe creativity is a way we can change things. For ourselves. And maybe through the power of sharing one another's creations we change lives?" Carly - My Mindful Journey @ CarlyJennings3

INNER UNICORN QUESTION TIME

How can being creative on social media help me get in sync with the universe?

How can creating content for social media be fun and playful for me?

Who could I hire or collaborate with to make it easier for me?

Chapter 10

CREATIVE CONSISTENCY

Consistency builds trust,
So being consistent with
your message is a must.
Being consistent with your tone, look and feel,
With showing up and sharing what is real.
This helps others connect with you,
Support you, know you, trust you -
It's true!

Clients often come to me asking for help with consistency, as it is an area a lot of people are struggling with. Consistency is an important part of your social media practice as it supports you in building relationships and engagement over time. It is when you show up consistently over time that people can get to know you / your message / your mission / your brand.

"Getting an audience is hard. Sustaining an audience is hard. It demands a consistency of thought, of purpose, and of action over a long period of time." Bruce Springsteen

Creating the content, and then actually sharing and publishing it on a regular basis is important for any kind of social media presence.

FYI: it's amazing how many will create content with the intention of growing their social media platform, but then not actually share it.

The good news is:

Consistency does NOT mean posting everyday anymore nor 5 times a day (thank-goodness!)

Consistency does not mean not ever taking time off from social media.

Being consistent can also go the other way. If someone is overly consistent, a bit over eager with their posting, I have found at times that I need to put a mute on that. Especially when it is not in alignment with where I am at in that moment and I am finding it noisy, or distracting - it can have a negative rather than a positive effect on my relationship with people online.

We are all in different cycles and seasons, when one of us is in our summer, someone else may be experiencing a winter. Getting into your own balance with consistency and trusting, knowing, **not taking it personally**, allowing for the truth that we are not for everyone, in every moment, also helps get our heads around our own consistency, confidence and flow.

Personal, subjective and unique.

I will share with you my process for creating a ***framework to flow within*** - one that will help you create consistency with your social media content creation and publishing, without the need for one of those big fancy editorial calendars that can feel overwhelming. This is coming from the girl who used to love a fancy editorial calendar. However, those times have changed and unless you are a big brand or a magazine or publisher, I have found that for most people managing their own social media, then a frame work is much softer and easier to manage.

First I want to share a recent experiment I ran on my own social media and a little bit about my own strategy for consistency.

As you should know by now, I believe that everyone's strategy and output is better if it is unique to them and to their goals, so this is not a strategy for you to copy, but more to give you inspiration and some proof of this in action.

We can so easily get caught up in thinking we need to do it like everyone else, but it is your Uniqueness that holds THE POWER – you are the key to your creative output and connection with your community online.

YOU ARE THE
CONSISTENT PART
TO ALL OF IT.

If you have taken time to explore your creative side and worked on your visibility vulnerabilities as per the previous chapters you hopefully will be in a place to be able to commit to creating content and publishing it consistently.

My strategy was to share something of value with my community through a weekly one minute video called a 'Social Media Angel Nudge'. Within a quick one-minute video, which is Instagram and Facebook friendly, I share knowledge, insight and expertise to serve my community and clients. It is something that I have been committed to now for a couple of years. It gives a one-minute nudge of insight into what it is like to work with me and addresses things coming up for clients and for the collective.

My nudges are consistent in their title, including the very popular (if I do say so myself!) opening where I nudge the screen:

This is unique to me and recognisable in the timeline. I may not get thousands of views but I get emails, messages, comments (and more often than not outside of social media) from all sorts of people I'm connected to, who tell me they watch and enjoy my nudges, even when they don't engage directly with them on social media itself.

Creating the nudges **gives me consistency** because I know have a solid format that I can produce easily and create regularly plus it

gives my community consistency in which to know me, my work. Hopefully they learn or get something from it which helps them too. It helps me to research and hone my ideas, it helps my paid clients and it helps me get more paying clients too!

Everyone's consistency will be different. I have been watching a few different accounts recently of women who are able to really show up, share themselves, their lives and their thoughts through their social media platforms. Author and writer Laura Jane Williams @superlativelylj is one. For me personally, there is no need for me to show up as consistently as she does, or share in the way that she does. It works wonderfully for her, she is very natural in this space and it is so much in alignment with her work in the world, so it works beautifully.

The beauty is in the variety and the diversity that is ever present online. If we can stop ourselves from spiralling off into comparison, stop looking at what everyone else is doing and thinking that we should be doing it like that too, then we have a much better chance of owning our lane.

Another potential consistency blocker is our addiction to numbers…

Growing a platform and follower numbers has been (and still is) a big focus for many people. People come to me with their spreadsheets (and expectations) tracking how many followers they gain and lose on a weekly basis, measuring their success (and their worth) based on that. This includes comparing themselves to other people's follower numbers and feeling that they are not succeeding because they feel they *should* have X thousands because Doris over there does.

Firstly, we don't know how anyone else achieved their follower numbers. Follow bots, click farms, big advertising budgets, influencer friends and so many factors can help create big follower numbers. One thing I would love to see change in this new age of social media is people shifting valuing their worth based on follower or viewer numbers to the value they are providing for people.

This is the world that we still live in though, from event promoters to publishers, follower numbers still mean something, and can be make or break in getting a gig or a contract. It makes me sad when someone comes to me who is very talented at what they do, but not very talented at social media, and feel they are unable to take things to the next level of success - unless they make social media work for them.

Even well-respected authors with big platforms don't always get the kind of numbers that are expected of them. I was watching an Instagram Live with Danielle la Porte recently where only sixty-five people were watching live, and I was surprised, and realised I was making a judgment based on the number of viewers she had. Now, I doubt Danielle La Porte is going to let something like that stop her from showing up consistently, but you just don't know.

Measuring our success on social media in this way has become second nature to most of us and it can be very interesting and useful at times. Insights (which we get for free on Facebook Pages and Instagram Business accounts) are a great tool to help you see what kind of impact your content is having and with whom.

I am not saying don't measure or watch for trends around engagement with your content - but start to look at ways you can measure your results in a way that doesn't affect yourself worth and doesn't stop you from trying new things if something isn't working.

Look also to if someone left you a comment to tell you how much that helped them... If someone reached out to you personally and shared a similar story or insight?

The measuring of numbers can (due to expectations and that social media ego of ours) get in the way of creating consistency. When we measure our success based on likes and shares, and we aren't getting a lot of those, we can get despondent and feel like we are failing, which can stop us from creating and from sharing. We get tired of not getting the results we expected, so we give up and stop.

You never know who you are helping, what connections you are creating, what magic you are manifesting - irrespective of the likes, shares and comments!

I find that when I share something, particularly something a little vulnerable, that I find myself checking, checking again, almost as an impulse - particularly in the first ten minutes after posting - to see how many likes, comments, views it has. And I find myself questioning the value of the sharing when it doesn't set the internet alight!

However, I have personally gotten much better with this by bringing awareness to it. Simply taking a breath and noticing my pattern of behaviour and choosing to back away from the mobile phone and allowing the share to do its magic in the ethers.

It is in the sharing consistently and learning to adapt (iterate) based on the responses (or lack of) that we grow. So rather than needing it to be perfect, use your social media platforms as a play-mat to practice getting in touch with who you are, what you do and with your message.

And now I mention it, perfectionism, that is definitely another consistency blocker!

I am not a perfectionist, but I do know a few (!) and have had some perfectionist clients. I know from speaking with them that the need to get it right or perfect before posting can really get in the way of creating consistency with their social media sharing.

In fact, for many of us, it leans into that feeling of being exposed, of vulnerability when we share and it's natural to want it to be perfect.

"Too many people spend too much time trying to perfect something before they actually do it. Instead of waiting for perfection, run with what you've got, and fix it along the way…"
- Paul Arden

Like anything you want to get good at, you do have to actively commit to the process, and start before you feel you are ready or before it is 'perfect'. So, if you want social media to be a key part of marketing and communications activity for your business, for your project, then you have to get over all of the above and find a way to show up for it.

A LOT of people see social media as this instant magic button to instantly connect to the world and make their businesses boom. I remember being in a meeting once where someone said, *"just stick it online and it'll go viral"*. Going viral is not as simple as sticking something online (unless you actually are Beyoncé.) And in fact, it's probably harder than ever now that platforms like Facebook are actively working towards connection over consuming passive content.

From someone who has worked in social media for over a decade, there isn't just a magic button you can press that creates a successful social media presence. It takes consistency and commitment to create, grow and sustain a platform and community.

It does takes time, work and patience – it is a marathon, not a sprint.

I understand that it can be hard to prioritise content creation especially when other things get in the way, such as running your business,

seeing clients, holding classes and workshops....
Especially when the rewards are not immediate
or in your face, like all those ads promise you.

As discussed, the success can be much
more subtle.

When you throw some resistance into the mix
it is easy to get stuck and not move it forward.
But if you don't create the consistency, it will not
improve. So I would invite you to sit with any
resistance you might have and explore that and
ask yourself, where is it coming from?

What is getting in my way?

Am I resisting social media?

If so what or where is the resistance?

Resistance can be due to many, many factors
that we have explored in previous chapters and
as always it will be unique to you. Identify where
it is and get support if that is required. Again,
there is no quick fix.

If you are ready, ready, ready to get
more consistent - here are a few more
suggestions for you:

*Remember that the quality not the quantity of
your content is important.*

*Think about what the value of what you are
sharing and why are you sharing it.*

Consider these things when thinking about your content and social media plans. And then create a content plan. Create a framework to commit to (coming up in the next chapter).

Take it a week at a time, until you can look at it a month at a time. E.G. I will commit to posting x1 video a week or x1 blog once every two weeks that speaks to, supports and connects me to my community both offline and online.

Let the consistency do its magic.

Enjoy the playing,
Enjoy the creating,
Enjoy the connecting,
Enjoy the journey.

INNER UNICORN QUESTION TIME

Where do I struggle with being consistent on social media?

What does comfortable consistency look like for me?

What is the intention for my post and for my social media as a whole?

Chapter 11

A FRAMEWORK TO FLOW WITHIN

A framework gives structure and strength,
to connect people on the same wave-length.
It ends the inconsistent yo-yo,
that makes content so-so,
Allowing the feminine to flow,
with the creative spirit of a rainbow.

Much like creating your social media strategy, creating *a Framework to Flow within* will help you create consistency with your social media content, presence, and publishing. The framework can form a key part to your social media content strategy.

I have found that it is best for most people to have the masculine structure of a frame work whilst simultaneously allowing the freedom and feminine creative flow to flourish. It is a balancing act to create consistency and content that is authentic and connects to your reason for being online in this way.

A lot of people come to me with no structure or strategy in place for their social media. I find that the *framework to flow within* gives them something to work with that plays to their strengths, creates consistency in their message as well as in their content creation, and community building which isn't too overwhelming.

Do you remember when I mentioned that...

"Facebook are "1% finished" and have a rolling strategy to keep improving through ongoing testing and feedback."

Having a *framework to flow within* helps you keep your strategy and content iterative and fluid. It can help those amongst you that are a "planner" type personality as well as the ones among you who have a "make it up as you go along" social media style. I have worked with each and this is a nice meet in the middle, that seems to work for a lot of people.

To create your own *Framework to Flow Within*, first of all get clarity on why and what you are using social media for. If you haven't already - sit down and write yourself a list of all the reasons you are on social media.

E.G. For me it would be something like this…

To share my ideas, wisdom and knowledge of social media on social media.

To create awareness for my ideas, my services, products, workshops, collaborations.

To help people and support people (community, clients & beyond) through my content.

To support those who are overwhelmed or stuck with social media in lots of different ways, by making it enjoyable, fun and spiritual.

To support the emergence of a new age of social media and marketing.

Now you have a go:

To become consistent we need to practice, play and enjoy creating content and showing up on social media. It is a practice and it can be a spiritual practice. One of my long-time supporters, Ruqayaya Daville sent me this message;

"I have had an amazing revelation that social media is more about a retrospective sharing of my soul... So when I choose a theme... and pay attention to that theme... it is a way of spiritually growing... Rather than the mindset of I have to do it because I need to show up... it has now started to become a spiritual practice." @ruqayyadaville

Much like Yoga or meditation are a practice, we need to get on the mat or on floor, sit it out or stretch it out if we want to build up our strength and flexibility. So too with our social media practice.

My Framework to Flow Within process:

The first thing is to make a commitment to showing up online with your message, your skills, your service.

If you feel resistance to this as discussed - meditate on it. Go back to those questions I posed in the last chapter and reflect here.

Take three deep breaths and allow your resistance to show itself.

See what comes up.

If it is a classic case of not feeling good enough sit and write a list of all the reasons you ARE enough…

EG. My clients think I am awesome.

I have experienced success with X,Y,Z…

If you are struggling with that, reach out to some clients for testimonials or friends and well-wishers to help boost your self-esteem. If you are starting from zero - tune in to why you have decided to start this in the first place and your reason for being online.

Remembering that ideally social media is a place to extend and reach out with what is already real in the physical world, that the digital dimension allows us to connect with others and share what we are doing in the real world with other people all over the world, through the use of the technology.

Therefore, you want to start with what is happening for you **in the real world** - in order to create your *framework to flow within.*

What is unique about the way you do the thing that you do?

If you haven't by now, let go of any attachment to the numbers - do it, do it, do it right now.

FOCUS ON CONTENT AND CONNECTION

Allow things to blossom in their own divine timing. Things take time to build and connect and sometimes you need time to grow into it. It only takes the right person to see one post, to offer you that gig, or that collaboration or recommend to you to someone, to bring about the thing you dream of.

It might be one post that changes someone else's life for the better in ways, you will never know - so drop any judgement. nb. Clearly if something continues to get NO engagement over time then you need to review things.

Drop into your heart and your social media soul.

The next step in creating your framework is to find **some key themes and topics for you to play with.**

EG. For me I look to what is coming up with my clients and the questions I am always being asked or the support that people are looking for -

In fact, one of my biggest tips to keep **in consistent alignment with your message is to be led from what is REAL in your day to day.**

EG. Consistency - this comes up time and time again for clients.

Therefore, this is a topic that you will find me riffing on quite often in my social media angel nudges.

Write a list of 2-4 key themes that come up in your work with your clients and in your business.

What are the topics that you are having conversations about offline?

What are you often talking about with friends, family, in groups or other?

What do people come to you and ask you about?

What are the things you are always explaining for people?

Those are great areas to tap into for social media content.

These themes will form a key part of your *Framework to Flow Within.*

Consistency is not just about how often you post but also what you post about. There is so much noise online that you want to be able to attract the right people into your circle, you want to be sharing with people that will engage with you and your work.

With **community, conversation and connection** a core value for the social media platforms moving forward, how can the content you create on a regular basis create those three things?

Next you want to decide on frequency and content types to add to your framework - the frequency of these content types is down to WHAT FEELS GOOD, easy, do-able, manageable for you to commit to.

Content types to choose from include:

Pre-recorded video
Live stream
Blog post
Micro blog
Promo/marketing/shout out
Podcast
Meme

Remembering that you do not have to post every day for people to get to know, like and love you - that quality over quantity is important here.

Play to your strengths when it comes to content creation but also think about how you can stretch yourself into the more uncomfortable stuff. E.G. video, or for a lot of people, LIVE video (I even get nervous for people when I see them go live).

Take that list and start to build out your personal *framework to flow within.*

A good framework for me would look like:

X1 pre-recorded video at 1min length for my Instagram per week or per fortnight (Social Media Angel nudge or other)

X1 blog / micro blog (relating to that video ideally) or relating to something coming up in the collective / with clients per week

X1 shout-out of content I am creating with a client, or for a workshop, collaboration or other thing to promote

X1 podcast - recording & publishing monthly but sharing content from weekly.

X1 Facebook or Instagram Live per month - Live is out of my comfort zone and committing to one live per month as part of my frame work would help me become more consistent with it. Ideally focused on the topic of the podcast for that month or around something I am promoting, a chapter from this book etc.

That gives me at least 4 posts per week that are in alignment with what I am doing in the world, why I am showing up and what I am looking to attract in terms of opportunities, conversations, clients and beyond.

Going back to the list of topics you created earlier, you can start to map out some series ideas and titles. People need / like consistency with a title, topic, look, feel, colours, fonts - all of the things - for them to recognise your content in their timelines and connect with it and build a relationship with you and with it.

When I decided I wanted to create a podcast to support this book and body of work, it made sense for it to be called *"Conversations on Social Media for A New Age"* where I chat to people on certain topics relating to this conversation.

That is a hook, a touch point, a consistent piece of content that people can recognise and connect back to me.

My client, Karen Ruimy, has a personal daily writing practice where she speaks to the Goddess energy and asks her questions. We decided to use these as the basis for her blog posts, where the Goddess would often come through with information that we would then share online. Karen wrote a book a few years ago called *The Voice of the Angel* so to tie everything together, we started to create some wisdom cards for an app which is called "Goddess is Speaking".

When we decided to create a podcast series this year it made absolute sense to call it "Goddess is Speaking" and use artwork that we have created for the app for the podcast itself – we made this title and this artwork recognisable with Karen's community and audience and linked content and products together too.

So, think about titles for the series of content you want to create - it helps to think about the ways that it ties into the products or services you are creating or wanting to build awareness of.

As part of this piece, I also use something called The Four Intentions created by Helena Holrick @ helenaholrick when planning out content ideas. When Helena introduced me to them it was a revelation and has become something I have been working with and sharing with my clients over the past couple of years. Everyone who learns the process finds it an incredibly useful tool not just for their social media but for their business and their life!

Because Intentionality has energy, when you set intentions for yourself and for your audience it helps create more clarity in creating your social media content and with creating better results. In a nutshell though I recommend you do this for each of the pieces of content you are thinking of creating as part of your framework to flow within.

Power of Intention

The concept behind the Four Intentions is that by looking closely at your own intentions for yourself and for your audience (customers, clients, tribe etc.), you can get really focused and clear on what outcomes you want to achieve. This helps you with what you create - be it a video series, a book, a workshop, a service or your social media strategy and content. By writing down your intentions you can save a lot of time and energy - not just with the clarity it creates - but also with the more magical frequency and law of attraction it brings to things.

My intentions for me.

My intentions for my them (clients, audience etc.)

"In the universe there is an immeasurable, indescribable force which shamans call intent, and absolutely everything that exists in the entire cosmos is attached to intent by a connecting link." – Carlos Castaneda

I am not going to lay out Helena's exact system here in this book, but you can listen to us talk about The Four Intentions in one of my **Conversations on Social Media for a New Age Podcast** which is free on iTunes and Soundcloud.

INTENTION IS POWERFUL

The late, great Dr. Wayne Dyer thought so, so much that he wrote a whole book about it!

"You get what you intend to create by being in harmony with the power of intention, which is responsible for all of creation."
- Wayne W. Dyer, The Power of Intention: Learning to Co-create Your World Your Way

This is one of the reasons why setting intentions for your social media content and using them in creating your framework to flow within is so powerful. When we create our content consciously with intention and share it with our communities, we are actually sowing these seeds of intention with every post we publish, drawing things to you through your commitment to showing up and sharing in this way.

By showing up with that content consistently on a weekly basis it is like setting an intention even deeper because you are putting regular energy into the space. And that energy is then allowed to expand, and it attracts, and it expands. It's like law of attraction in action through your social media.

This makes us become much more conscious to what we are posting and why we are positing it and where the post is coming from, rather than just posting aimlessly. One of my clients was feeling a bit disappointed about the results she was getting in terms of tangible results through her social media platforms, so I asked the question, *"did you set any intentions/goals for what you wanted to achieve?"*

If you don't set an intention or goal for what you want to achieve with your social media, it is easy to get despondent and think that it is not working, or forget to be strategic about how you set about achieving what you want.

So we came up with some goals for the next few weeks together - e.g. X4 more coaching clients and x10 reviews of her book. We then came up with a couple of ideas - *a framework for her to flow within* - for content and connection that she could develop and action - based on these goals and intentions.

I hear so often from people that want / need to be on social media, who are posting rather aimlessly in the moment (I do it too!!), but without any kind of framework to support the work, and so it is then really easy to become a bit frustrated with what appears to be a lack of results.

Take a moment at some point to sit down and write a list of intentions for you and for your audience - what you want them to receive, or be able to do as a result, and what you would like them to feel.

Get clear on your:

Topics
Content types
Publishing frequency
Series ideas and titles
Intentions

You now have a *Framework to Flow Within*. Now get creating, and make it happen!

Most people find that creating space for content creation on a weekly basis is the best way for them to commit to their content framework. It might be that you keep Wednesday afternoons or Friday mornings clear for content creation for that next week ahead. There you record your video, write a couple of micro blogs, and posts, set up the interview for your next podcast or edit up and prep the one you have ready for publishing. By setting this time aside it helps you find your flow - through the consistency.

You can batch your content creation and prep a week's worth of content in a couple of hours a week - avoid being sucked into the *"what on earth am I going to post today?"* scenario that so many people find themselves in.

When we view our posts, with our content as planting these seeds of intention in order to allow our dreams and goals to manifest, the intention behind the content creation from concept to creation becomes such a different process - an enlightening, ever-evolving, process of clarification and manifestation.

INNER UNICORN QUESTION TIME

What is unique about my mission and about me?

What seeds do I want to sow and how can I sow them through my content?

What framework can I create to let my creativity flow within?

Chapter 12

AUTHENTICITY, VULNERABILITY & MARKETING

Authenticity is so HOT right now,
Being vulnerable too,
helps us connect,
share our know-how.
But when it is done
just for marketing sake,
Then it feels fake.
Do we always have to be on the take?
It's time to awake.

"The savvy modern consumer demands quality and authenticity."

@adweek

"Authenticity" has become a big buzz word for copywriting, for sales pages, posts, ads, lead magnets, and for social media in general. This has now spilled into 'vulnerability' being recommended as a top marketing and sales technique too.

To quote social media business coach, Alex Tooby @instawithalex who posted this recently; *"Vulnerability and authenticity are two really powerful concepts that can lead to major success on Instagram. (I'm talking far more engagement, more clicks on your links, and yes more money!)"*

It makes me feel slightly crazy. Why? I can feel people now 'trying' to be authentic and being extra and overtly vulnerable because they have been told / it has been proved that it will help them build their social media platforms, their engagement and their sales. This is why.

Sometimes I see a post and I think how a friend wouldn't necessarily share that much information with me over a coffee - let alone someone I don't know personally on the inter web. We've all seen those posts where we wince a little and think 'ok, ok, TMI!'

There are times when this is good, when the big vulnerable sharing is helpful, when it is genuinely vulnerable, and that vulnerability is really helping others through the act of sharing, through its bravery and its truth.

If you have ever read Bréné Brown's *Daring Greatly*, there are so many quotes I could draw on from her about the power and beauty of vulnerability.

"Vulnerability is the birthplace of love, belonging, joy, courage, empathy, and creativity. It is the source of hope, empathy, accountability, and authenticity. If we want greater clarity in our purpose or deeper and more meaningful spiritual lives, vulnerability is the path."
- Brené Brown, *Daring Greatly: How the Courage to Be Vulnerable Transforms the Way We Live, Love, Parent, and Lead*

When it's done from that place, it can transform lives. But when it's not, when it's only being done as a marketing technique, then we have to ask if it is authentic. We would do well to lean into our own discernment when it comes to what we see on social media, because people are using and abusing this.

As content creators, I recommend keeping a check that we don't tip from genuinely sharing ourselves and being authentic or vulnerable with our audience because it demonstrates something of importance about our experience, and our connection to our cosmic consciousness... To doing it only BECAUSE we have been told to do it as a way to get results.

Tamara @wolfsister kindly shares more of her thoughts on authenticity and vulnerability on social media here;

"A lot of people coach, teach, practice as healers/ intuitives because of what they have been through in their own lives and they're implementing their own methods or tools regularly, but we're all still figuring it out. Which to me is authentic. I believe it is good to be transparent and people need to see that it's a journey. I don't share vulnerable posts to get people to want to work with me but like I said; for me it's about transparency and connection."

In today's now age of social media, because we have data that proves authentic communication gets more engagement and helps build relationships, this has become a bit blurry.

So let's explore this one together. It really is new territory. As with all social media, we are now dipping in and out of each other's lives via devices in our hands and we are being given ways to reach and share in ways we have never have before.

And it's so new in the world of marketing and advertising that we are bound to find this one a bit tricky as we are all learning how to navigate this with our integrity intact, without falling for the gimmicks but still being smart and using the tech and tools for our businesses, to sell services and products, to attract clients et al.

"I think that it's a really beautiful place to be exploring; vulnerability, authenticity, intention, tenderness, and compassion in action. And then also; being in the unknowing, you know, being in the unknowing, of what this is. And then being the witness, being the witness to everything as well, whilst maintaining playfulness, fluidity, flow state and being in the vortex, at the same time really. So I'm delighted that there's a chapter on this. I think it's going to be really beautiful. I think it's going to be really rich for people. I think we're just at the beginning of this aren't we? In terms of what any of it means. On or offline. Such an interesting topic, and I very, very much look forward to speaking to you more about it."
- *@gail_loveschock*

You can listen to Gail in another of my podcasts riffing on using social media as a marketing and sales tool for her business authentically rather than being authentic as a sales and marketing technique for her business. You get the difference?

I think one of the most important points of difference when leaning into this is our **'Intention'.** And as per the previous chapter, our intention is powerful.

"Authentic: of undisputed origin and not a copy; genuine."
- Google Dictionary

Authentic means genuine, real and true. GENUINE authenticity and vulnerability is needed in our world of masks and mirrors. It is time that we see beyond the perfect 'highlight reel', that we are able to be OURSELVES and show up and share our different facets - the shadows as well as the shiny.

It's when we try too hard to be authentic that it feels yucky. In the same way we can feel the energy and intention behind people's posts, we can also feel when someone is being authentic and being themselves or if they are doing as part of a cleverly crafted marketing campaign.

This is part of the shift into social media for a new age.

Into the age of Authenticity, into the age of Aquarius.

Authenticity in the Algorithm

"One of our News Feed Values is **authentic communication.** *We've heard from our community that authentic stories are the ones that resonate most – those* **that people consider genuine** *and not misleading, sensational or spammy."*

"For example, if Page posts are often being hidden by people, that's a signal that it might not be authentic."

"We will now take into account how it signals change in real time. So now if there is a lot of engagement from many people on Facebook about a topic, or if a post is getting a lot of engagement, we can understand in real-time that the topic or post might be temporarily more important to you, so we should show that content higher in your feed."

- Facebook News Room

The faster people respond, and the more people respond at the same time, the further the content will reach, no matter what the content is, because the algorithm understands this as being important to you and to other people.

This is how things go viral. It is also how content can go nowhere just as fast. Really it comes down to whether or not the content makes people **FEEL** something. The more of us that feel it and express that feeling through our engagement - the more people will see it.

Ask yourself does your content, or do YOU, make people feel or think in a way that they might want to express that through their engagement with you online?

But not in a click bait kinda way.

Headlines that 'bait' and 'trigger' you to click by exaggerating or distorting information is something Facebook are actively trying to stop. 'Fake News' is another big issue here and it is something we should also be looking out for too.

According to BBC Newsround, there are two types of Fake News.

"False stories that are deliberately published or sent around, in order to make people believe something untrue or to get lots of people to visit a website. These are deliberate lies that are put online, even though the person writing them knows that they are made up. And stories that may have some truth to them, but they're not completely accurate. This is because the

people writing them - for example, journalists or bloggers - don't check all of the facts before publishing the story, or they might exaggerate some of it."

But how does or can an algorithm really know what is true and what is false?

The manipulation of images, videos, people who straight up lie and post disinformation, fake reviews, comments, fake figures…

I watched a <u>vice.com</u> video, *"I Made My Shed the Top-Rated Restaurant On TripAdvisor"* where a guy who had previously been paid to write fake reviews for restaurants decided to do an experiment.

"Writing fake reviews on TripAdvisor. Restaurant owners would pay me £10 and I'd write a positive review of their place, despite never eating there. Over time, I became obsessed with monitoring the ratings of these businesses. Their fortunes would genuinely turn, and I was the catalyst."

He then decided to create a fake restaurant and see if he could get it to No.1 on the platform.

"And then, one day, sitting in the shed I live in, I had a revelation: within the current climate of misinformation, and society's willingness to believe absolute bullshit, maybe a fake

restaurant is possible? Maybe it's exactly the kind of place that could be a hit?"

Oobah Butler for vice.com

And he did. It is a fascinating case study as to how things can be manipulated online.

How do of any of us know what is really the truth?

The fakery, the bullshitting of all kinds is rife in the online world… From my days in the music industry I remember how much it is at play in PR and in the media…

Basically, in the world.

Some humans lie.

Some people are very good at it.

Did you ever watch that show on MTV called Cat Fish?

"Cat Fish: Someone who pretends to be someone else, especially on the internet. Found on anywhere from Instagram to Twitter to chat sites, these people use fake pictures to disguise who they are."
- Urban Dictionary.

Turns out a lot of people create fake profiles and date people for months, nay YEARS, all under a false identity! Crazy but it happens a lot.

It is very real, even though it is very fake.

In this modern age of social media people can seem authentic when in actual fact they are not. Discernment is paramount. Pick who you follow or friend wisely. Learn how to pick up on the energy of the posts in your feed.

If something feels off...

TRUST that feeling.

If something feels like they are just leading you to a click, a like, or a sale...

TRUST that feeling.

If something makes you feel bad more than it makes you feel good...

TRUST that feeling.

MANIFEST
DON'T MANIPULATE

I do feel a bigger conversation needs to be had about how digital marketing and sales strategies are used particularly in the mind, body, spirit and wellness industry, which includes soulful and conscious entrepreneurs and businesses who are focused on people's well-being, on relationships, on spirituality as well as on profit.

For me, countdown clocks are a personal bugbear.

Yes, they work as a technique to "help people make a decision", but we need to dig under some of the psychology as to why they work. My opinion is that they work because they create a sense of urgency. How does urgency feel in the body? For a lot of people urgency feels like stress.

"You have 3 days,1 day, 12 hours, 1 hour, ONE MINUTE people you have ONE MINUTE and then this offer will magically disappear into a puff of smoke… Never to be seen again. UNTIL the next time I decide to offer it… Possibly next week. Or maybe even tomorrow. Actually, I'll reopen the cart for an extra 24 hours to drive some more sales before I really close the cart - but make sure you don't miss out because I may never ever, ever offer this again, and if I do, it will be double the price, and then you will be sorry, or broke, or depressed, or alone for eternity… or dead… or something."

When I started to tune into what my body was saying, rather than what my mind or emotions were doing, that's when I really started to wake up to what some of these forms of marketing were doing to me, to us. People disagree with me on this one, because some of us (and this has been proven) need this bit of urgency to make a decision, to 'push people over the finish line' to purchase, but I still feel there is another way outside of a second by second tick tock clock.

Yes, remind people, let them know what you are offering, and have deadlines where they are needed, but don't stress people into it.

I was recently on the sales page of an author I know and respect, when I noticed there were six countdowns on the one sales page alone. Each time I encountered the clock, I noticed it sent my nervous system into a spin, with its sense of urgency fluttering in my stomach.

The marketing and sales landscape is a minefield of manipulation. NLP (neuro-linguistic programming), psychological tricks and beyond have been used on us for years (basically since the 1950's when advertising industry started to boom) to get us to buy stuff, so why would we expect anything else in this our modern, digital age?

It's what people have been 'taught' to do, and told to do, in order to be a 'version' of successful and I'm not sure we even question it. It's another place where our patriarchal programming lays dormant. And it does work - so businesses will continue to use it, until we actively start using our personal power and not buying from companies who manipulate us in this way. I'm not sure that all of the businesses that are using it are even consciously aware of the energy it carries.

I guess the questions we can ask our inner unicorn when deciding on how to market our business, our services, our products is this:

Is this in alignment with my ethics and way of being in the world?

What is my intention in using this marketing method?

I have even heard of spiritual entrepreneurs (thankfully none that I know or work with) manipulating clients using their intuitive, empathic and magical skills to create sales. Sometimes it may be unconscious, but using energetic hooks to pray on vulnerability for business purposes does happen, so it is good for us to be aware of that.

I actually got this unsolicited direct message on Instagram recently;

"Hi would you like a reading? I went through your profile and I picked up on your energy, I feel you have been feeling confused and are at a crossroad, I don't usually DM people only ones

I know I can read for. Let me know if you are interested."

For most of us, I hope the thought of doing that would be a resounding "NO".

Katheryn Pearson, an HSP (Highly Sensitive Person) who teaches teen yoga, EFT and who is helping parents understand high sensitivity, messaged me with her words of wisdom around authenticity, vulnerability and marketing.

"When we talk about "sales and marketing techniques" do we need to rephrase what that means to us? Is there stigma around "sales and marketing techniques"? Are all sales and marketing techniques bad?"

She continues;

"We know that being authentic is what builds community and connections. Showing up and being ourselves is what we are being asked to do. I purposely don't be authentic to sell... I am authentic and that seems to sell. If we tell people they can't use authenticity as a way to make money... then how do we make money? I think we are being called to share more, face our fears and put ourselves on the line... I certainly have felt as though I have put myself through a lot to be this authentic and help people. I hear a lot "bravery is rewarded" from my guides. The

main point being... I don't be authentic to sell in a sneaky way... I mean, can you even do that? I'm authentic and I'm rewarded for that."
- @katheryn_pearson_

Not all sales and marketing techniques are bad, but some of them are not great. I personally think we are doing a disservice (creating karma even??) by 'being sneaky' with our marketing. How do we flip reverse the lack mentality methods to an abundance mentality to create a myriad of thriving for all?

Energetically and spirituality it makes more sense for our New Age does it not?

I have worked with a number of people over the past few years where we are selling digital products or digital events and making GOOD money (tens to hundreds of thousands) without a countdown clock or a pain point in sight. They do have big audiences and they provide good, regular free content and cultivate their communities.

As I understand it, with a lot of these digital marketing methods, you are to some degree playing the numbers game. Which is why the big numbers on a list matter. The higher the numbers, the higher the clicks or emails you have in a list, then the better chance you have of converting enough % (even it's a small %) of those clicks into sales to make money.

When the focus is on the numbers, on the formula, on the clicks, and not on the people, I feel we lose some of the humanity and authenticity behind a product or service.

Having spent a lot of time and money on digital marketing training, as well as my own 10 years+ experience in the space, focusing on numbers didn't resonate for me, nor did it come easily to me or fill me with joy. Quite the opposite. That does not mean that it does not work for whom it comes naturally and for those that love it… And I am sure there is a way to do it well and do it ethically… I know you exist! Please tell me about it, share it with us all. #socialmediaforanewage

But I also know lots of you on the other side of this; where this feels untrue, where it creates a sense of lack, of burn out and of not being good enough. People that have spent thousands on training, that have put it all into action and still come out the other side without the results they were often promised.

I like to think of myself as a social media angel super hero for a new age… A not so secret social media vigilante.

The reason I am calling some of these marketing practices out is because of how they make us feel. How do they feel to you? And how has your relationship with a person or a brand changed because of them?

I was noticing that it no longer felt good for me, or for a lot of people that I am speaking to and quite frankly the feedback is that many of us find it boring and have now switched off. Just like the advert breaks.

I think a good example of this to share is Marie Forleo's B-School. When B-School went really big in 2014 / 2015, the affiliate scheme was something we had never seen before. The marketing, the launch, they were as slick as they were successful. Everyone who was anyone, (or who wanted to be someone) were talking about, or were, an affiliate to B-School. After a couple of years of that, the affiliates alone were enough to drive me bonkers. It felt like every post in my timeline, and every email in my inbox was someone offering their 'B-School bonus' at the time of the launch (due to my social media bubble), and that is when things switched, it went into over-kill. I spoke openly about it at the time, and I got a lot of messages from people sharing how it made them feel, how they had unfollowed and unsubscribed from a LOT of lists because of B-School promo.

The other thing about something like B-School, is that in teaching SO MANY people in a similar field how to get started, how to set up their online space, it has created a cookie cutter generation of B-Schoolers where everyone's stuff looks and feels the same. They use the same techniques and tools which has made things a little bland in social media land, in all its shiny-ness.

Of course, this isn't just limited to B-School. People are getting bored of free summits, webinars, sign up for free video series and 'lead magnets' of all kinds. In a way, the sheer volume of people doing their marketing this way has de-valued a lot of it. Of course, it depends on where your audience is at, how exposed they have been / are to a lot of the same kinds of marketing and if you are pushing your edges and evolving with them.

A recent increase in adverts and sponsored posts in my Instagram feeds and Stories timeline, prompted me to ask my community how these were making them feel…

"Overwhelm on speed."
"Very annoying. The energy feels sharp."
*"Feels intrusive and like I'm not on
my own phone."*

*"Feel myself losing interest in my
feed already".*
"So, so annoying".
*"Messing with my mojo - I feel like they
broke Instagram"*
"Less feed - more noise."
"Invasion of my personal virtual space."

Sponsored posts from a very wide range of businesses, people I know, people I don't, products, coaches, weight loss, accounting, banks, fashion... Every 4-5 posts there is now a sponsored, clickable, call to action post. And what I've noticed is that the energy is often very different in the posts people have chosen to spend their money on and promote.

Again, I'm not saying that boosting or advertising on social media is wrong, I'm simply asking the question:

How does it make us feel?

How is it making our customers and clients and friends and contemporaries and connections feel?'

I do not want to add to anyone's sense of feeling 'annoyed, hijacked and overwhelmed'. It's not how I want any of my content to make anyone feel, organic or sponsored, so what can we learn from this?

How can we evolve from here?

Of course, it must be working, businesses wouldn't be investing money into developing or delivering something that isn't proven to work. Although from what I hear, results can never be guaranteed, even from the slickest and most expensive of agencies.

There is a reason we like to watch *Netflix* and pay for streaming with no ads. There is a reason we like *Spotify premium* and not the ad version. There is a reason we don't like pop ups, or even want to look at banner ads. Half the time it's because they are a bit shit, (I watch TV sometimes and can't believe that what I am seeing is for real when it comes to the ad break) other times it's because we're no longer interested in hearing about things we don't want.

Sound off. Pause. Forward wind.

Video content and infomercials is the current trend on social media but is it right for everyone?

Now, I want to add a disclaimer here, because remember my pre-cog activity from 1996? I do tend to see and feel things before they happen when it comes to online stuff. And the feeling in my bones is that things are shifting and businesses big and small would benefit from looking at what the evolution of this is.

For me evolution includes more transparency, less formulaic and less interruptive.

"As consumers get savvier and have more and more options available to them, authenticity and transparency will become more and more important." @adweek

I am asking these questions for us all to make the enquiry because I believe it is important, particularly in my field of Mind, Body and Spirit, where you are talking to a community, a consumer, who more often than not is aware of what they are feeling or sensing.

Definition of Free

A lot of the messaging for marketing funnels, magnets and leads use the term 'free' which is another word that has become overused in the online space. It can carry a funny energetic charge in these times, because how free is it? Something to consider.

It's no longer a surprise for many of us when a sales pitch happens at the end of the free video series or webinar or summit, because it has been done so often. A lot us know that 'free' means 'opportunity to sell'. There is a reason people don't engage with promotional posts - giving something away for free before offering a product, can make us feel like we have been lied to on some level, especially if there has not been transparency from the outset. Even if we are not fully conscious of it, over time it effects our ability to trust.

"Is it free? And I ask this BC I AM TIRED OF FREE AND THEN HERE COMES THE... BUT THE PRICE IS... I am not expecting anything for nothing... But tired of the bull that follows. Just saying."
- @theantiquedistillery

This comment was in response to a sponsored post by Influencer @jennakutcher on a free download on 'how to build an email list'.

TRUST IS
SO VALUABLE
LONG TERM

So, to anyone using any kind of product launch formulas, I ask you to sit in meditation, or just in thought, and tune into the vibration of the marketing methods themselves and ask the methods some inner unicorn questions of their own...

Are you love or are you fear?

Are you abundance or are you lack?

Are you soul or are you ego?

Are you true or are you false?

Are you trick or are you treat?

The content and integrity of a person, or a product itself, could be wonderful and wants to be out in the world, but in this ever-evolving new paradigm, using the older (and yes, even a couple of years is old in this social media space) marketing methods which are now being overused, particularly in the online-learning sphere, means that wonderful things are not being seen, or experienced. A lot of people I speak to are sick of the sales and marketing emails in their inbox, the countdowns, the special offers, the cleverly crafted crafty copy. People are overwhelmed with the volume of them, they're switching off, unsubscribing, deleting them the moment they see them.

These methods don't feel authentic anymore and we feeeeeeeeel that on an energetic level, and so we no longer trust that.

I hear things like *"it's a proven sales technique, one recommended by my business manager"* when I approach people about it. Often the energy of it is not something they have really thought about, until I point it out. One recent such case was where I encountered a 10-minute countdown clock (!) to sign up for a special offer for a digital product about authentic copywriting which made me totally question everything and if anything about it had in fact been authentic.

And I get it - we are busy, and we hire people who get results. And this stuff does get results. But does it get results in a way that is in alignment with our soul? And how long can a model like this sustain itself in the Aquarian Age?

INFINITE
ABUNDANCE
AVAILABLE

Digital products are infinite, so when we use lots of 'limiting' tools to sell them it is not in alignment with its state of being.

Social Media for a New Age (and business and marketing for a new age) is about finding ways to market and sell consciously, successfully, abundantly without the need or use of these old paradigm methods.

I love this from Madeline Giles, creator of Angelic Breath Work and fellow lover of all things Avalon, she shared on her Instagram stories recently about selling places for her Heartfelt Dreams Retreat in Mt Shasta:

"Last month when there were three sign ups, I prayed about it and Spirit said to connect fully to my heart, rewrite the retreat copy from my heart, and let go. Let God. I listened and now one month later it's full. I am so grateful to serve by practicing and experiencing what I share. It is the greatest honour of this life! Listen to your heart, it knows".

- @madeline_giles

I think some of the problems arise when we feel we are reliant on just using online marketing and sales to make a living, particularly when starting a new business. People are often sold the idea that they can make six figures fast, live the laptop lifestyle and travel the world without having to do the work.

By all means, get familiar with the structure of a formula or a function (like sponsored posts), feel into it, ask it some questions, listen into what you can learn from it and what parts of the process feel good; then drop it.

Write your sales copy, Instagram posts, books, content and everything in-between in a way that comes from you, that like Madeline, comes from your heart. This way, you will attract the right people to you, to your work and to your life in a way that will be enjoyable for everyone.

The power of a good word.

Word of mouth and referrals are still a very powerful (if not the most powerful) part of marketing. And let us not forget being online is social networking not just social media.

The rise of the freelancer, solo-preneur, entrepreneur, laptop lifestyle, work-from-home era where Wi-Fi and 4G allows us to live, which is a life I love living, by making money online, is more popular than ever before. I've seen co-working spaces popping up worldwide with digital nomads roaming the planet and running their businesses online. What I witness is a big increase in people setting up a pretty website and Insta grid, growing a following or group, without having the experience of actually running a business, producing a product or really knowing who they are and what they have to share. And yet, they are giving the impression, through their well-put-together social media, that their business is very successful when actually, they're not.

I saw someone from one of the co-working spaces on my travels recently own this reality check…

"I was broke af. At first I did have clients, but it was unsustainable and I didn't enjoy it. It's a lot of desperation, learning on your feet, hard work and a shit ton of luck I guess. Most people are faking it too, I'm sure".

Personally, I am not reliant on just social media and digital marketing to create leads for my services. In fact, I am not sure that I even want a business that looks like any of the current business models I see out there. Having an office-based business didn't suit me. But I am not sure that a slick, fully automated digital product-led business suits me either. My business is about an integration, a juxta point between my experience and knowledge with my real world and online connections, community, relationships and my social media is about sharing about that. This is where the magic really happens for me and for many of my clients. We have lost sight of the need for real world substance behind a pretty social media feed or sales funnel. That stuff is in many ways the easy bit - years of working, training, learning, developing your skills and your craft - that is the depth, and so are the relationships; and that is the part we can expand from, learn from, or buy from.

Is it all in the list?

Digital marketing people say that *it's all in the list,* aka your Email list. A lot of importance has been placed on the size of your email list as a marker of success. But in this new age of social media - is it all in the list?

Or is your social media platform just as, if not more, powerful than an email list for your business?

I have been playing, exploring and researching different experiences and people's feelings about their mailing list and about mailing lists in general, and I want to share a couple of different scenarios with you so that you can decide for yourself how important it is for YOU to spend time and energy building your email list.

One reason the email list is considered so valuable is that you own the data and the emails yourself, rather than being at the mercy of the social media platforms who own your followers and your 'contacts'.

"Here's the deal: I'm paying for you to see this. Why? Because you are worth it and also the truth of the matter is that less than 6% of the audience I've hustled for is actually seeing what I am putting out into the world. Crazy right? So, if you're starting to realise that social media is just borrowed space and it's time to invest your energy into something you OWN, listen up! My email list is #1 way I drive profits into my biz and chances are you've thought about starting one but you're not sure how you'd even get people to sign up. I put together 8 easy ways for you to grow your list (even if you are starting at 0). Grab the free guide here… "

- @JennaKutcher

Jenna is a social media influencer, who shared this in a sponsored post for a free guide that takes you into a sales funnel for a course on Growing Your Email List… (Just sayin')

She makes some good points. Organic reach is lower for businesses and publishers on promotional posts. This being at the mercy of the social media platforms of course means being at the mercy of the Algorithm, which I've tried to demystify for you earlier in the book.

And remember how MySpace went from being the biggest thing to being tumbleweed in no time at all?! It can happen. And I for one am watching as the Facebook data scandal unfolds to see what this will mean for their platforms long term, and if people will indeed #leavefacebook.

The importance of the email list, however, made much more sense to me when emails used to always get into your inbox. In this day and age, a lot of emails from mailing list providers end up in Junk or filed away through tools like Microsoft exchanges 'Clutter' tool, which learns what emails you open and which you don't and files away the ones you don't. Meaning much like the algorithm; the content that matters most, based on your actions ends up in your inbox.

It also made more sense when email was still the most direct and intimate way to contact someone online, but this has all changed SO much in the last couple of years. I get messages on WhatsApp and Facebook messenger that feel much more personal than email does now.

This is why marketing through chat bots on Facebook Messenger has been launched recently - but with AI robots doing the talking, I'm not sure if that is going to work (for my business anyway!) – perhaps for bigger companies using it for customer service enquires et al, but not so much for solo-preneurs, individuals or smaller businesses. I have seen a few people using this tech, and their inboxes are swamped with the weirdest messages coming in from people that think they are speaking to someone real when actually it's a bot.

Again, not very authentic unless it comes with a disclaimer.

It reminds me of when I was working in the music industry and we were managing social media accounts for popstars and replying to fans under their name. The fans would get so excited if they got a follow, a reply or a retweet, not knowing that it wasn't actually their idol doing it, it was either someone's team or a follower bot.

Email and social media platform numbers are considered a true marker of popularity and viability especially by traditional publishing houses or brands, so if you are looking for a publishing deal or a brand partnership the number of subscribers on your social media and your mailing list can and will make a big difference to getting a deal. It was the same in the music industry, if you wanted to get played on the radio, YouTube views and Twitter follower metrics really mattered, even though they could be manipulated or bought.

You need to measure how important the numbers are for you in this context, when looking at your business plan and your goals.

The value of an email contact used to be placed very highly by marketers, but I really feel that this has changed in the current landscape. I have 5 email accounts, and one that I use specifically for signing up for free content and mailing lists so that it doesn't impact my day-to-day inbox.

The ads we see on social media about building your mailing list quickly through a "lead magnet" (a freebie that people will exchange an email list) doesn't always mean results for your business, your products or your launch.

I have a client who came to me for support in building connection and community on her social media channels. She had invested in a Facebook ad campaign which would be considered a success. She built her email list into the thousands with targeted ads for a free webinar. However, despite the high sign up rate, she had very few people show up for the webinar and consequently, the sales of her product launch were much lower than she had expected or hoped for.

It has been seen that simply building an email list is no longer the answer to our digital marketing dreams. The landscape has shifted, particularly for a conscious, aware and discerning audience.

Whether it's an email list, a Facebook group, a Facebook page, an Instagram account or Twitter feed - it still comes back to the relationship you build with the person on the other side of the screen as being the most valuable.

We want to build trust; we want to build relationships. I understand that the automated email sequences are designed to build that relationship over time… BUT we have also got **very used to,** and **bored with,** the same kind of emails that have been filling our inboxes for years. I would say that we have got **email fatigue.**

I do think it still has its place for certain industries and for certain people. And I am not dismissing the huge successes that many people have had through their email list and through using the varied product launch formulas that are out there. I just know that through my work they are not for everyone and that there are other avenues.

In a recent coaching call, one of my clients told me that it felt like a massive weight on their shoulders - building of the list - and was actually creating tension and blocks in her flow to building community on her social media platforms.

I also feel that the constant requests for us to "sign up to my email list", creates a disconnect on social media.

I have noticed myself sighing loudly when someone is constantly trying to get me onto their list before they have built a relationship with me through their content.

"Would you have sex with me without foreplay? No. No you wouldn't. Because I wouldn't let you. Same goes for this."
- @sassylisalister

It feels like we have become a world obsessed with getting someone's email address, and it's not sexy.

BALANCE

I'd love to see more balance. We absolutely should be making people aware of our offerings, our products and actively looking to build our platforms either on social media, on email or on both - in fact I had a call with a client today where I was telling her she needed to do this more often! But we don't need to do it every day or on every post.

We are often made to feel like having a big email list is the only way to make our business thrive online. I read something recently on Mashable, *"No updated email list, no online business – that's just how it works."* And we are in interesting times with the European Union new GDPR (General Data Protection Regulation) for data which means that everyone now has to update their mailing list and/or privacy policies… This is giving a lot of people the opportunity to opt out of and leave mailing lists that no longer serve them. I have a feeling mailing lists will shrink significantly due to GDPR and it's a good thing for us all to have an opportunity to clean up databases and to only be in communication with people that want to be there.

So, is having an updated mailing list the only way online business works?

The belief that the email list is the only way to succeed online creates a lot of stress for people. It definitely adds to some people's social media vortex of doom. Remembering that email is just another platform or communication tool, helps me with this.

Think about how you use your mobile, what apps are you hopping between when you are unconsciously tapping? Usually it is two or three apps, does it matter if it is email, Instagram, Facebook, Messenger or WhatsApp?

Yes, you can market and automate things differently through email sequences but again it comes down to the relationship. And as discussed, those relationships are in some cases being damaged by email marketing.

TIMES HAVE CHANGED

One way out of this particular vortex of doom is to be more flexible and fluid with the "ownership" of your contacts - you may have me on an email list, but it does not mean that I open your emails, that I like you, that I trust you, or that I am going to buy something from you. Yet, I may follow you on Instagram, or Facebook or YouTube and the moment you offer something I am going to snap your hand off for it. Or, if I realise I need a product or a service you offer, I will seek you out because you are the person I think of for that 'thing', because I have built an authentic relationship with you over time that I didn't need to be 'funneled' into.

I think we should give our audiences more credit (and respect) for knowing what they want, like or need, and that they are more than capable of finding and going to your website if they are really interested in working with you or buying something from you.

Sometimes it feels like the only reason someone is doing social media is to try and get you to go somewhere else, to a mailing list or a YouTube channel or to a website. Rather than connecting with you right there where you are, where they have your attention. They forget that the person they want to communicate with is right there in front of them, on that channel or platform. If you are doing this, please stop trying to lead us somewhere else to tell us something - do it right there in that space, in that place.

Rant over.

INNER UNICORN QUESTION TIME

If I am being authentic or vulnerable as a marketing technique - is it still authentic?

What do I like or not like about other people's marketing on social media or in my inbox?

How am I using my platforms to build or maintain a relationship with my community, my customers or my clients?

Chapter 13

CONNECTED COMMUNITY

Connected Community
is marketing for a new age,
and so much more.
And these turning points,
they turn faster
Than they have ever turned before.

If 'comm' is short for communication and unity means "the state of being united or joined as a whole," then social media is by its very nature - **community.**

I watched a TED talk; *"The secret to living longer might be your social life". The Italian island of Sardinia has more than six times as many centenarians as the mainland and ten times as many as North America. Why? According to psychologist Susan Pinker, it's not a sunny disposition or a low-fat, gluten-free diet that keeps the islanders healthy -- it's their emphasis on close personal relationships and face-to-face interactions."*
- YouTube TED 2017.

Much of our social lives and connection to our communities are now in this digital age happening through social media and social networks. Although it might be digital - there are plenty more "face to face interactions" and "close personal relationships" happening because things like "FACEbook and FACEtime...

When the connection through these platforms is authentic and real, there is the potential for us to see social media as a tool for increasing our connection and personal relationships with our closest people as well as through our online communities.

COMMUNICATION THAT UNITES US

Social media unites (and divides) us in many different ways. I was talking with my friend Henrietta @henrietta_sacredleaderhip about the language of energy and how powerful social media is for connecting us with our soul tribe.

OK get this.

I met Henrietta @henrietta_sacredleadership in a Facebook group led by my dear friend Jen McCarty @jenfinmccarty. I met Jen a couple of years ago, online, initially through her blog. Henrietta and I were in one of Jens zoom groups and were in Bali at the same time. We met up there and became instant buddies. One year later, Henrietta flies from Australia to Glastonbury, because she has received a calling from content she was seeing me and others post on social media. Henrietta is a grid worker and works with different energy points on the planet; photos or videos from people and places around the world really affect her. You can hear her talk about this process in one of my Conversations on Social Media for a New Age podcasts.

The same happened with Kaja @Kajavibes and Maja @Majametlicar who run the Irresistible Tribe. We were all connected through Jen, and Bali, and social media, and we have been friends online for a couple of years now. They messaged me to say they were also coming to Glastonbury and asked could we meet?

A connected web weaving between the physical world and the digital world, our mutual connections, our communities, able to connect and gather in person, to work together with the land and with each other.

That wasn't about clicks and conversions.

But social media for the win.

Funny that the word 'conversion' is so close to the word conversation. In fact, conversion and conversation are just two letters apart - add AT to conversion and you get conversation.

CONVERSATION IS WHERE CONVERSION IS REALLY AT

The most impactful things that have happened for my business through being on social media have been through CONVERSATION. Real ones, with real people. Those conversations have come through connections and through community. Old fashioned real-world connection and networking - done digitally and physically.

So, when I get asked the question, *"How do we/I/ you create community on social media?"* my first response is to tell people to look to the people you actually know or like, to look to friends of friends, colleagues, clients, connections and start there.

We have a real network and community right under our noses on social media that we often overlook the importance and value of, in pursuit of the big numbers. Perhaps it is too simple to think to start where we are, and with who we know or to who we want to know.

LOOK TO WHO YOU KNOW.

When thinking about the promotional strategies for this book, rather than thinking of ad campaigns and sales pages, I have been thinking about who I can naturally have a conversation with, where and in what way online or offline about what is in the book.

I am saying yes to all the Insta, Facebook live chats, podcast interviews, guest teacher slots that I am being asked onto and I will reach out to other people too. I would rather be introduced to and **have a conversation with** a connected community and make an impression or an impact that way. I know this will be way more effective and enjoyable **for me**, than spending hundreds or thousands of pounds programming sponsored posts or ads.

It is often overlooked because we think we have to have thousands of people following and liking our content on social media, with these automated email sequences and scheduled posts doing the work for us, to make an impact.

When you get to a certain level and are reaching people into the tens, nay hundreds of thousands or millions, then an integration of these tools becomes necessary, and can still be done with integrity.

But not everyone is in that position yet.

I know from the conversations I have on a daily basis with clients and connections, people are craving another way of doing business online, or feeling there is another way to do business online, and still be successful.

And for me community is where that is at.

Talking to your own community on your channel, on their channels, expanding organically through the power of love, connection conversation and good old fashioned social media networking.

Success doesn't have to look like the big six-figure launch. It doesn't have to look like anything else anyone has done. Success could look like working three days a week, whilst making 3k a month, or being able to take a month off and your business thriving because of it!

Real connection and community in your life both personally and for your business is about the strength of the relationship, the strength of the container that that relationship it is held in - be that online or offline.

Mark Zuckerberg says that Facebook's products are about connecting people. *"Facebook is about bringing people closer together and enabling meaningful social interactions; it's not primarily about passively consuming content."*

Because of this, 'Community' is becoming *another buzzword* on social media due to the attention it is getting, and the changes to the algorithm to give more prominence to groups. We have to be careful about how we interpret this as it can become another social media stick we beat ourselves with. The *"I'm shit because I don't have an active group"* stick.

*Tip: You don't have to have your own Facebook group if you don't really fancy running one, instead be active in other peoples. Especially ones where you know who is running it. That is my current group strategy as I don't have time/ energy right now to hold space for my own group and I am honest with myself about that.

So, if we are looking to Facebook in this instance and what it wants to stand for - which is to *'bring people closer together'* and to *'enable **meaningful social interactions'*** - how can we use social media for this purpose for ourselves, for our lives, for our businesses?

It doesn't mean you have to run out and set up that Facebook group, although this is better than a Facebook page in terms of the algorithm right now, **it is about the container that you create** and the community you invite into that space, which isn't limited to Facebook Groups.

To make this concept of community and connected community easier and more manageable, rather than seeing it as somewhere to connect with thousands of people, start by seeing it as place to connect with peers, clients, community, people that you know, that know you and grow your connected community from there...

You are not speaking to all two billion people on social media, you are not Beyoncé, remember? ;) It doesn't need to all be about YOU. It can mean creating a space and a place for people to connect with each other, a fertile ground for growing connections for all, be it around a topic, a mission or simply a sacred space for sharing.

I helped Nicola Berhman @7om_alchemy come up with the idea for her 7om Temple of Illumination Facebook Group. The space is magic, it is a container for connection, and

Nicola holds that space energetically as well as digitally.

Another great example of a Facebook Community Group is 'The Event is Happening'. Jen @jenfinmccarty set the group up to support her community, friends and clients learn about something called 'The Event', as she was getting lots of information about it from her spirit guides, and then started seeing loads of other stuff about it online.

In just eight weeks the group grew to over 20,000 members, all completely organically! I was one of the first into the group and watching it grow has been a beautiful case study for me. So many of my friends started to appear in there as the weeks went by, without me adding them in. And from the get-go everyone was sharing photos, insights, articles, visions, dreams and more; all with the intention of supporting each other and the planet. It was amazing to see this happen before my very eyes! Jen did a Facebook Live in the first week and invited me on to speak with her and to the group.

It was community, connection and meaningful conversation right there in action and I loved being part of it. Jen was asking me about social media and *what part do I think it plays in relation to The Event?'* I was able to share what I know and at the same time I was connecting with a wider group of people. We are constantly connecting with like-minded people that know each other offline as well as online by being active, authentically on social media, and we have no idea as yet where those connections may take us.

By doing the Live or saying yes to other opportunities to have **conversations** with people online, I am raising my profile. As is Jen by running the group. I am pretty sure that by being in service, setting up and creating a space like this, Jen and all the others who decide to show up in leadership in this way will be rewarded, without needing to sign everyone up to a mailing list or capture everyone's data.

"Bravery will be rewarded"
- @katheryn_pearson's guides.

The power of human connection is so strong right now. And as Alexi Panos and creator of *Soul School* posted recently *"in a world of algorithms, hashtags and followers, know the true importance of human connection"* @alexipanos

One of the problems I foresee with automating everything with the sole intention of marketing something, rather than connecting and creating community, is that as we become more and more emotionally aware and intuitive (which I believe is happening to all of us on the planet right now to some degree). We are able to read the energy behind emails and posts, that anything inauthentic or contrived, is becoming much less impactful over time.

It already is.

Creating community and a sense of love and trust with your people, taking the time to build relationships through great content and access points (eg Facebook or Instagram Live). Having, or creating, conversations to make an impact online and offline so that people trust you and want to attend your retreat, hire you as a coach, spend time reading your book or coming to one of your events.

Connected Community for Introverts

It's harder to create community when you are an introvert or you don't know how to use the tech. I understand connecting with lots of people online can be overwhelming and takes confidence.

I have noticed something about my own social media habits when exploring this. I can be quite shy about posting in groups or on posts and am having to break through a wall that I hide behind. Even though most people think I'm a confident extrovert, I am also a shy introvert. One of those extrovert/introvert types.

I will post content and ask questions and have an expectation of people to comment and answer, or for there to be lots of engagement but I will then shy away and hide when I get lots of comments and connection, but isn't that what we all crave? Yes, we crave comments, but when they come, we can't, or don't, actually reply to them all.

Passively posting content can be so much easier than actually talking to people. But, if we want to create community then we have to actively engage on some level, especially taking into account where we are at with our online/offline profile.

It can take time, but it really is something you can actually make happen. It is somewhere you can grow. It's important to have boundaries and get away from social media as I've talked about, but being active on social media allows me to basically carry the world and all the communities I'm connected to around in my pocket. It allows me to connect online throughout my working day with colleagues, clients and friends. It's a web of community and connection that supports me every day.

When I was getting over my shyness about speaking out and showing up, it was by remembering that I actually know a lot of the people in my network, that many of them are my friends or are colleagues or connections of friends, friends of friends. Because that's how many of us connect with each other through social media. We meet at a work thing, we friend request or follow. We see someone commenting so we friend request or follow. I speak to a lot of people on social media that I know in this way and am constantly meeting now in real life. It's so wonderful.

Another community building thing to consider is this:

I made a commitment to spending some time leaving comments for the people I know; cheering on my clients, my friends and my community when I see them stepping into their power, into their confidence, sharing their voice, their skills and their creativity... Sharing their hearts and their souls with me and everyone on social media. I know how much effort and bravery it takes to create and publish. I know what people go through to really, honestly and openly share themselves on social media. By commenting or liking – even if it's just a thumbs up - I know it means something to that person and it is helping their content reach further.

"Kindness Improves Relationships - This is one of the most obvious points. We all know that we like people who show us kindness. This is because kindness reduces the emotional distance between two people and so we feel more 'bonded'. It's something that is so strong in us that it's actually a genetic thing. We are wired for kindness. Our evolutionary ancestors had to learn to cooperate with one another. The stronger the emotional bonds within groups, the greater were the chances of survival and so 'kindness genes' were etched into the human genome. So today when we are kind to each other we feel a connection and new relationships are forged, or existing ones strengthened."

- Dr David Hamilton from his blog *The 5 Effects of Kindness*

I look at who looks at my Instagram stories, I take notice of who is liking and commenting on my posts and I know that they are the nucleus of my social media community and they are important to me. So, I like to share that love and make that effort and be there for them and for others too, through the act of liking and commenting.

It means so much more to our social media soul when we know that person. That is how we consistently build relationships over time through social media. Through that connection.

Birkan Tore @birkantore is someone I have been connected to through social media over the past year through his friendship with Diana Cooper and Tim Whild. Birkan is an intuitive life coach and has a TV show called 'Saved by the Angels" with a big following on Instagram. He posts Angel card-readings and recently after hurting his wrist, decided to do his card readings on video, which was new for him.

The comments were full of people saying how much they loved this new format as one said, *"so lovely to hear and see you"*. I left a comment for him too, he replied…

"Thank you for the feedback and encouragement. It's funny that I have a TV show but I'm freaking out about making videos…"

I feel like I know Birkan better and have connected deeper through that one meaningful interaction.

We can't create a digital community for ourselves without actually connecting, communing and conversing, so we have to get over ourselves and stop hiding. Silently hoping that we will create a community without having to do anything, or through automation, isn't really going to get us there. For automation to work there still needs to be a relationship created somewhere!

So here are some inner unicorn questions to ask yourself when exploring the concept of creating a connected community on social media…

Are you wanting to create community because it's the 'in thing' right now?

Why do you want to connect with more people on social media?

What is your intention and purpose for this community?

What purpose is it serving outside of marketing a product or service?

Does your community have to exist within a Facebook group? Or could it exist through your profile, page, on Instagram, WhatsApp or somewhere else completely different?

Do you get involved in other groups or comment on other people's content?

Do you leave comments or send DM's and start conversations with others?

Creating a successful community online for your business or your mission starts with partaking in communities that already exist on social media, and is a great way to practice. When you don't have the experience or even have the desire to really be on social media… *What needs to shift?*

Spend time exploring and being on social media to find the right place for you to create this sense of connection and communication. Shifting any limiting thoughts and feelings about social media in order for you to use it as a tool, as technology, that allows you to connect with others more.

Rather than feeling like you have to be something or someone else online, trust that the very act of connecting and communicating on social media as yourself (in your tone, your voice, as you would offline or with friend, that by getting involved in real conversations online, by commenting, being in groups, by being part of other communities) will in turn help you create real connections with real people and increase this sense and feeling of real community.

If we are in our social media ego and feeling like we have to show up as this elevated version of ourselves, or in a disconnected version of ourselves, it is harder to create a real sense of meaningful connection.

The passive consumption, that way of doing business online is going through a turning point.

It worked for a long time for those at the top - from the mainstream media and the digital marketing industry, and for the big named entrepreneurs and brands.

But for the thousands of people coming online, seeing social media as an opportunity to make a living, be independent, to pay the bills and live their lives, to support their dreams...

People in their sovereignty,
Conscious people living their dharma,
Earning money through living their passions,
Healing people through their arts
and services.

People living lives, wanting to use the internet better, to use social media more efficiently and more productively to promote their passions, connect with others and create abundance in their lives. Where technology and social media is about supporting them **as simply as possible.**

INNER UNICORN QUESTION TIME

Am I creating a group or community because it is the 'in thing' or because it is the right thing for me?

How can I use a sense of community to create meaningful social interactions?

Who are the people I know that want to be in a community of like-minded people, focused around my mission?

THE EPILOGUE

There is so much to do,
But when we stay true, to our inner guru,
That's when we make a breakthrough.
So share from the heart,
Express knowledge and art;
Let that be your part,
And watch it fill up your cart.

Social media can be a joyful, artistic space for creation, connection and self-development as well as a space for conscious marketing, business networking and promotion.

Remembering that it is multilayered and operating on many, many levels and dimensions, energetic and otherwise, can really support you in taking your social media to the next level with this approach.

My big hope and wish is that this book helps you feel reassured that being on social media is about so much more than simply 'likes' and 'follows'. It's about connecting with your global soul family, finding your voice and sharing your magic and medicine with others. It is about raising the vibration of the planet with content that helps one another, whilst helping ourselves by sowing the seeds of manifestation for our own goals and dreams.

When what we post affects and activates us all on a daily (hourly??) basis it is wise to acknowledge its power, be it through messenger, Facebook groups, Instagram et al. The digital dimension is leaking energy into and from our physical bodies and lives.

We are using it to change the world, especially when we choose to show up in service, with intention and purpose more often. Using it more consciously, we are massively supporting a wave of awakening, using the internet like a Mexican wave of love, information and ideas spreading around the globe.

WE ARE THE WAVE
WE ARE A WAVE OF CHANGE

Social Media is one of the training grounds for multidimensional living, for learning how to be and connect with the hive mind daily. A super consciousness that can help change the planet for the better. It is supporting us in creating a shift - that is undeniable. It is up to us, each and every one of us, to show up through both our digital and physical footprints.

Big Data is proving how powerful our hive mind is and this is only going to become more important as artificial intelligence develops. We are indeed the ones who it's learning from, through our use of technology to upload information second by second.

It has huge, and potentially dangerous, abilities to control the masses too, as seen in the news where millions of Facebook profiles were mined for data and used to target people with political propaganda.

It's real, big stuff and we *have* to look at it.

If you are not awake to this, then it is time to get woke and learn more. The internet and smart phones are creating an evolution and revolution of our species and lifetime. Getting wiser and smarter about how we are using it and how other people are using it, is important and necessary.

I am not perfect at this. I've not always checked data policies and I use social media in ways that are not always healthy, be it addictive checking or endless scrolling and I need to get better at setting clear boundaries with it so it doesn't consume so much of my time and energy. But when I focus on creating time, space, structure and strategy around how I am using it, I am always rewarded.

It's such an amazing and wonderful tool; it's like having a magical device from the future in my hand. I mean, it is freaking amazing what we can do that has evolved in the last ten years.

What is this all going to look like in another ten years' time?!!?

Information passed between us, broadcast via a thought wave? No more need for stooping over a handheld or laptop device… (yes please!) Our brain will be the device (but without the need for implants and weird mess-with-your-head stuff either please, thank you).

WAIT a second.

Isn't that what is happening to people during meditation? Monks, priests, shamans, channellers, seers, witches and psychics have been doing that for centuries!

"Technically, Moses was the first person with a tablet downloading data from the cloud"
- Unknown via @gail_loveschock

This meme quote popped up in timeline as a nod of affirmation; and that's another thing that happens, getting synchronicities, hits and signs in my social media timelines. If you hang out in some of the places I do, the chances that one of your friends, someone at the table or on the yoga mat next to you will be getting a download, transmission or activation from an angel, spirit guide, past life or a someone they met in a Facebook group or on Instagram is pretty high.

Viewing it in this new way can help us to shift;

The frustration into fun.
The wasted time into time well spent.
The unconscious scrolling and comparing
into consciously creating valuable content,
conversation.
To owning our own lane,
*within our own **personal, subjective and**
***unique** global communities.*

I didn't say it would be easy - but this is part of our life now, and it's part of our evolutionary puzzle. I am so grateful to social media for the part it is playing in helping us to create a new paradigm.

We are so connected, and we are so loved.

To wrap up, I'm going to share some love and gratitude for social media and a few of the awesome things it brings to my life. I'd love you to do the same and for you to share them with me online via: #SocialMediaForANewAge

"Love and gratitude are identical vibrations.
Appreciation is the vibration of alignment.
When you reach it, it will pull you toward all of
the things that you consider to be good in a very
powerful way."
- Abraham Hicks @abrahamhickspublications

Offering this vibration of gratitude to the platforms, to the medium, can create some overall loveliness, and if you are feeling a bit cynical about this social media for a new age malarkey, then I would recommend this even more! The social media magic happens daily and when we notice its magic and we thank it, when we tune into all the magic in our lives because of it, more magic happens.

INNER UNICORN GRATITUDE TIME

Social Media rewards me through the meeting and deepening of relationships with others.

I was in Thailand when I saw on Instagram that one of my old friends from my music industry days, @jonogrant, was doing a gig in Bangkok. We haven't seen each for years due to life, work schedules… The next day I see in stories that he has flown to Ko Samui for some R&R. I message him with an *"OMG you are on the next island to me!!!!"* We exchange messages and the next day I jump on a boat and meet him for lunch. We got to spend some real quality time together catching up, that was so special and all because of social media!

Social media rewards me through activating and initiating positive change in my life.

I have learnt more about what food I should be putting in my body and what foods to avoid even in the "healthy" section from the incredible Danielle Shine @chefshine on Instagram than from anyone. She shares so much great info when she is shopping in her Instagram stories and her recipes and insight are next level! Eating the right foods and learning about what is good for me helps me increase my energy levels and wellness that helps me be more productive and more creative! And we have become good friends thanks to social media too. Double win.

Social Media rewards me through positive feedback and conversations about my work and my ideas with people all over the world.

Last week I had a private message drop in from someone who said…

"Katie just wanted to say, when I see your videos and stories about not getting caught up in the pressure of social media I feel like you're such a voice of reassurance and it helps so much just seeing your content! It's so grounding and reminds me of what's important on this platform x thank you for what you do it is so important and so needed ♥"
- @soulspoon

I was blown away by her message and it gave me the confidence that what I do is needed, which helped me finish writing this book.

Social Media rewards me with new clients and ideas for my business all the time.

Last year I received a message on Instagram following a post/nudge I had shared on the importance of "consistency". The message asked, *"do you provide a service to help with consistency?"* At the time I didn't, so I thought about it and decided to create one. From this my Social Media Angel Sister Sessions were born. A three-month package where I would be there to help people create a strategy and keep consistent over three months (with a view they can do it themselves from there). I had space for five people to do this with, posted about it the following week via Instagram.

No sales page, free webinar or anything complicated just an invitation to email or message me to find out more. One week and two posts, it was sold out. Everyone that signed up for the sessions I already knew through social media, even though I hadn't worked with any of them before.

Reflection

Having the opportunity to reflect on some of these moments with you, and throughout this book, has shifted my relationship to the medium even more deeply, to realise and recognise its role and value to me across many parts of my life and to shed some of the conditioning I have been carrying around how I **'should'** be using it.

Social Media for a New Age is in part a personal journey of discovery, with its multidimensional ways weaving between the physical, the spiritual and the digital, an exploration of ourselves and each other, connecting through these different platforms and portals through our digital content and avatars.

I hope that it has provided healing and inspiration, as well as practical tips and ideas for creating and managing your own platform and having your own social media adventures.

As we start to experience and talk more about our individual and collective social media ascension symptoms, we recognise that change is always happening, and we get to choose how we use social media in a way that feels good to us, and for us – not just in a way that drives clicks, likes and follows. I'd love this book to be call to action, a conversation starter, an iterative evolution instigator.

If you see people talking about things that make you think of *Social Media For A New Age*, or if you share your thoughts, ideas and perspective on social media with your community - please hashtag or @ me - I'd love to be involved in the conversation.

If this book has struck a chord,
Please help it spring-board,
And share the love on your platform or page,
#SocialMediaForANewAge.

See you in the timelines,
Katie x

ACKNOWLEDGMENTS

(AKA LOVE NOTES AND THANK YOUS)

A big heart felt THANK YOU in this
book, my debut.
For your love and support
Has been a divine consort,
Which has helped me stay true.
I love you.

Firstly, big love and thank you to myself for doing this. And to my higher self, etheric support team, faery, unicorn star friends & family who are all doing big rainbow glitter dance moves in the ethers right now. We did it.

Lisa your friendship, hand-holding, editing and role in birthing this book has helped bring my ideas and my mission to life beyond words, or ways I can type. THANK YOU for helping me do this and for being my friend.

Sean, I'm so proud of all you are doing with That Guy's House, for helping authors, for making it easy and enjoyable. I am grateful to you for helping me share my work in the world in this way.

Mum and Dad. You are the best. I love you so much. Thank you for bringing me into this world, always loving me, supporting me and my off the beaten track, slightly crazy ways.

Huw, for always listening to me and my stories. And for helping design the cover. Thank you for being one of my besties in this life and beyond.

To all my loves near or far… Those who have journeyed with me and supported me in different ways over the years (and some) … Natty, Chris, Kat, Ruthie Ann, Morgan, Nicki and all the girls,

Ryan, Helena, Becky, Cari & Frannie (best villa mates!), Henrietta, Gail, Jen, Jdot.

To all the places and spaces, nooks and crannies, cafes, sunspots and grid points where I tucked myself away while I wrote this book. From Sunset Hill, Ko Phangan to Glastonbury Abbey, your energy and beauty inspired me.

BIG love and thanks to all my clients, those who I get to explore this with regularly and go on a social media, work, life, spiritual adventures with, especially Karen, Diana & Sue. I am so grateful to you for hiring me, trusting me and working with me in the way that you do.

To Hay House UK. Michelle, Jo, Diane, Amy & Tom for introducing me to so many wonderful authors and working with me across the years.

Sandi your support delivering for clients has given me the space I have needed to get this book written. I appreciate and value all that you do for us.

John and Gaia, learning about energy, about flow and how to say 'F**k It' in all of the ways CHANGED MY LIFE. And continues to change my life. Without you and your work, I would not be who I am today, and I wouldn't have been able to say 'F**k It' and write this book in the way that I have done. Much love and respect to you.

Dani, I love the social media Angel and unicorn SO MUCH – thank you for collaborating, adding to this experience and to this book. And Peter, thank you for your care, patience (and speed!) in getting the book to look how I wanted and out into the world.

Sarah, we met in a social media for a new age kind of way just recently and have only just started working together but thank you in advance for all that you are going to do to help me get the word out.

And last but not least to everyone I meet/hang out with/am supported by on social media. To Lucy, George, Kathy, Nicola, Greta, Tara, Karen, Rebecca, Danielle, Kelly Ann, Claire, Emma Louise, Kate, Kitty, Jade, Helen, Darlene, Alex, Kimberly, Theresa, Faith, Nicola, Hannah, Tamara, Rachel, Ciara, Shannon, Sophie, Tamsin, Eliza, David, Jenny… to name a few… your comments, hearts, chat and love do not go unnoticed.

And to everyone that buys it, reads it, thinks about it, is inspired by it, posts about it, shares it… THANK YOU for reading, listening and enquiring.

ABOUT THE AUTHOR

Clients call Katie Brockhurst their "Social Media Angel". It is more than a nickname: It's a job description, an ethos, a mission statement.

A social media consultant for leading international Mind Body Spirit publishing company Hay House UK. Katie has worked with many of their authors including Diana Cooper, Sonia Choquette, John Parkin, Dr. David Hamilton, Yasmin Boland, Rebecca Campbell, Kyle Gray and Lisa Lister. Plus many other well known authors, practitioners and businesses in spirituality and well being.

From London, England with a solid background in broadcast, music and entertainment, working for Sony, BMG Music, BBC Radio DJ Dave Pearce and Wise Buddah Talent. Katie started her own social media agency 'Kdot Online' in 2007, when the social media in- dustry was in its infancy, after winning a Gold Sony Radio Academy Award in the first ever Best Internet Programme (podcast) category . Kdots client projects included O2 Music, Universal Music, Sony Music, Penguin Books & Harper Collins.

Katie developed her business to match her own passions and life choices, and in 2014 she wrapped up the agency and the demands of running a London office in order to travel the world with her laptop, going solo as a consultant in the MBS industry, where she had established a name for herself with Hay House.

Katie now delivers 121 consultancy, coaching and strategy for authors and experts all over the world online.

She is loved for her simple, positive, actionable strategies that play to people's strengths and personalities, enabling them to find their passion for content creation in order to create meaningful community and results online.